SUNDAY ROASTS

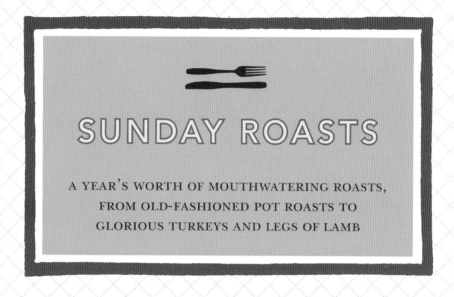

SUNDAY ROASTS

A YEAR'S WORTH OF MOUTHWATERING ROASTS,
FROM OLD-FASHIONED POT ROASTS TO
GLORIOUS TURKEYS AND LEGS OF LAMB

by BETTY ROSBOTTOM

PHOTOGRAPHS *by* SUSIE CUSHNER

CHRONICLE BOOKS
SAN FRANCISCO

Library of Congress Cataloging-in-Publication Data available.

ISBN 978-0-8118-7968-2

Manufactured in China.

Designed by Sarah Pulver
Prop styling by Randi Brookman Harris
Food styling by Maggie Ruggiero

The photographer wishes to say that working with talented, dedicated,
creative professionals like Randi (and baby Harris), Maggie, and Alaric
was truly a gift in every way. This was a project where like-minded people
gathered to eat, work, laugh, and create! It was a pleasure.

10 9 8 7 6 5 4 3 2 1

Chronicle Books
680 Second Street
San Francisco, California 94107
www.chroniclebooks.com

DEDICATION

For Mary Francis, Emily Bell, and Diana Tindall.
With gratitude for sharing your creativity, your talents,
and most especially your friendship.

ACKNOWLEDGMENTS

This book came to life because of my editor, Bill Leblond, who believed in the idea and did not let it die. Many, many thanks for your faith in this project, your guidance, and your wise counsel.

Lisa Ekus, my agent, and all her group, especially Daniele Mathras, gave me support and advice every step of the way.

No cookbook can be written alone. Mary Francis, Emily Bell, and Diana Tindall, my incredible kitchen team, spent hours helping develop and test the recipes for this collection. There are not enough superlatives in the dictionary to describe their dedication and friendship.

Mary Francis also put her stellar computer skills to use, moving documents and material from one virtual place to another with lightning speed. She also took charge of getting the recipes to the testers and then compiling their reviews.

Thanks to Debra Baughman of the National Cattlemen's Beef Association and to Mary Bartz for sharing their vast knowledge of beef cuts and roasting.

Sheri Lisak and June McCarthy, longtime colleagues, efficiently fine-tuned the recipes. They tried variations, kept careful notes on timing and temperatures, and made invaluable suggestions along the way.

A group of dedicated cooks spread across the country volunteered to test the recipes for this collection. Week after week, they carved time from busy schedules to cook roasts and side dishes and then offer super feedback (pun intended!). Thank you Wendy Kersker Ninke, Marilyn Cozad, Jackie Murrill, Ron Parent, Betty Orsega, Cindy Kurban, Marilyn Dougherty, Carroll Vuncannon, and Bob Corea.

Talented novelist Elinor Lipman helped me find the right titles for the chapters, while Ellen Ellis, a good friend and gifted writer, made my words sing.

Thanks to Sarah Billingsley, Doug Ogan, Sara Schneider, Tera Killip, Peter Perez, David Hawk, and the staff at Chronicle Books, who are warm, enthusiastic, and extraordinarily creative. What a joy it is to do this book, our fifth together. To Susie Cushner, Maggie Ruggiero, and Randi Brookman Harris, thanks for the beautiful photographs.

My son, Mike, and my daughter-in-law, Heidi, and my precious grandkids, Edie and Griffin, sampled roasts (many far from perfection) on holidays and visits to my house, rarely with complaint and often with helpful critiques.

My husband, Ron, deserves a huge hug. Night after night he ate roasts, often the same one several times within a week. He washed piles of dirty dishes, edited pages of text, offered psychological therapy when needed (often!), and best of all interrupted my worrying with one of his jokes!

TABLE OF CONTENTS

BEEF

PORK

LAMB AND VEAL

POULTRY

SEAFOOD

SIDES

SIMPLE YET SATISFYING PARTNERS
137

EXTRAS

**CHUTNEYS, RELISHES, SEASONED
BUTTERS — GREAT FLAVOR
BONUSES**
161

INTRODUCTION

The Art of Roasting and
Roasting Tips and Guidelines

"A Sunday well spent
brings a week of content!"

A PROVERB

Some of my earliest childhood memories have to do with a culinary tale, which became a legend in our family. It seems that in the early days of my parents' marriage, my mother thought that she should invite my dad's boss for dinner and decided to make roast duck as the main course. Her efforts turned out not to be promising. A new and totally inexperienced cook, she overcooked the bird, rendering it dry and tasteless.

She served it anyway, and the guest, a Southern gentleman through and through, tried desperately to eat the dish set before him. However, he had false teeth and could barely get down a single bite of the stringy fowl. Fortunately, my dad kept his job, and my mother learned how to roast. In the years that followed, she produced many delicious roasts of beef, ham, and chicken, but she never again pulled a duck from her oven!

Roasts were always special at our house whether they were for family or company meals, and I think that's true for most of us today. A roast is never an afterthought. And if in the past cooks (like my mother) seemed to only turn to that triumvirate of standbys—roast beef, roast chicken, and ham—that's no longer the case.

There are countless possibilities for what to roast today and endless ingredients that enhance flavor. In this collection, you'll find a chapter that features beef and another that highlights pork, two perennial favorites. Another section has pages devoted to roasting chicken and its interesting relatives—turkey, Cornish hens, and yes, even duck. Lamb and veal both yield cuts perfect for roasting, so you'll find a chapter that focuses on these tempting meats too. Another chapter is devoted to treasures from the sea, including salmon, cod, halibut, and tuna, which all take to oven cooking beautifully.

What you serve with a roast is also important, since side dishes should complement, not compete, with the star attraction. In this collection there's a useful chapter that includes familiar accompaniments with innovative twists as well as plenty of delectable new creations. There's also a final section that features recipes for robust chutneys, savory relishes, and seasoned butters—those essential little extras that make roasts of all manner shine.

Although you can roast on any day, Sunday is a time when many cooks have a few free hours at home, unencumbered by weekday work and schedules. What better way to spend part of that day than turning out a beautiful roast to savor with family and friends. And those leftovers—well, they are perfect for the rest of the week.

THE ART OF ROASTING

Whether you are roasting a pepper-coated beef sirloin, a big plump chicken brushed with herb butter, or a whole salmon side seasoned with soy and orange juice, delicious aromas are certain to waft from the oven and permeate your kitchen. These suggestive, fragrant scents, heralding the dish to come, are one of the reasons that roasting has not lost its popularity since the days when cavemen cooked meat on a spit. Roasting produces great contrasts in textures. The exterior of roasted foods is often well browned, even crusty on occasion, while the interior remains moist and tender. Anticipating what lies beneath the toasty outside is one of the great pleasures of a roast.

Roasting is an easy technique to master. You don't need to hover over a roast; once it is prepped, you place it in the oven, and it practically cooks itself. For today's time-deprived cooks, roasts offer another dividend. I often serve a roast one night and then use the leftovers imaginatively on another.

The word *roast* is both a noun and a verb. A *roast* is the piece of meat that is being cooked and *to roast* is the method used to cook it. So what constitutes a roast? Technically it's a piece of meat, poultry, or fish that is cooked in the oven and is usually large enough to serve more than one person. Although many roasts are cooked uncovered without any liquids, others profit from the addition of moisture. The ever-popular pot roast, for example, simmers in aromatic liquids and is roasted under a lid, as are roasted lamb and veal shanks.

What can be roasted? How long do you want the list to be? Meat, poultry, and fish are the wider categories, and within each there are different species and different cuts. Beef, veal, pork, and lamb roasts can be cut from the leg, the loin, the ribs, and the shoulder. Poultry choices include a variety of birds from the omnipresent chicken to turkey, duck, and Cornish hens, all of which can be roasted whole or in individual pieces. Many types of fish can be cut into large or small fillets and roasted. Even shellfish take to oven cooking beautifully.

ROASTING TIPS AND GUIDELINES

At the Market

Make a point of getting to know your butchers and fishmongers, and take time to introduce yourself so that if you call to place an order they know who you are. Even if you shop in groceries that sell prepackaged products, there are usually butchers and fish experts behind the counters. Strike up a conversation by asking them what is fresh and well priced that day.

In general, when purchasing meat for roasting, I prefer to have the butcher cut it fresh. However, if you are searching for a roast in the prepared meats section of a store and can't find what you need, don't hesitate to push that button for assistance. I can't tell you how helpful butchers have been to me on such occasions.

The same butchers who cut your red meat roasts can ready a chicken, turkey, or other poultry to your exact needs. When it comes to fish, the people at the seafood stand know what came in that day and can guide you to the freshest catch. Fishmongers are also great at recommending substitutions when the fish you had your heart set on is unavailable.

THE RIGHT EQUIPMENT

Pans and Racks

You don't need a lot of equipment for roasting, but there are some essential pieces. Basics include two good, heavy roasting pans, one large and one medium, with low sides. I like the enamel-coated cast-iron pans and stainless ones with an aluminum layer sandwiched in between for good conduction. It's best if the pans are flameproof, so that they can be set on the stovetop for making pan sauces.

Some roasts are best placed on a rack. There are a couple of basic types. One is flat and will function simply to keep a roast from touching the pan and allow air to circulate around it. The other is adjustable with sides that can be set to accommodate roasts of varying sizes. I prefer the latter, which I believe provides more support.

Thermometers

Unless you are a professional chef and can test for doneness by simply pressing your fingers against a roast, thermometers are a must. An oven thermometer will let you know if your oven temperature is accurate.

An instant-read meat thermometer will let you see what temperature your roast has reached. Instant-read thermometers don't last forever and need to be replaced regularly.

Tongs, Mitts, and Spatulas
For tending to a roast while it is in the oven, you need heavy mitts or potholders, sturdy tongs for turning, and wide, heavy stainless steel spatulas for lifting it out of the pan.

Kitchen Twine, Skewers, and Basting Brushes
For tying roasts and trussing birds, keep strong kitchen string on hand, and metal or wooden skewers for closing the ends of rolled or stuffed items. A basting brush will aid in brushing flavored butters and glazes on meat, poultry, and fish.

BEFORE THE ROAST GOES IN THE OVEN
All roasting recipes call for preheating the oven so that it will be at the correct temperature when the roast goes in. Count on 15 to 20 minutes for the oven to preheat. If you have time, it's a good idea to let meat roasts come to room temperature for 30 to 40 minutes before roasting.

Roasts (with the exception of those that are marinated) are usually patted dry to remove any excess moisture, then seasoned. The seasoning can be as simple as salt and pepper or as complex as a spicy rub. In some recipes, the meat or chicken or even fish is sautéed for a few minutes before it is placed in the oven. This pan-searing will produce a light browning on the outside, which adds extra flavor and texture to the roast.

Large birds need to be trussed, a simple technique that involves tying string around the perimeter of the fowl so that it holds its shape and will roast evenly.

WHILE THE ROAST IS IN THE OVEN
Roasts need to be kept moist once placed in a hot oven. Those roasts that have a generous exterior coating of fat or plentiful interior marbling get basted naturally as this fat melts. Other roasts will need some help. You can brush them with seasoned butters, baste them with stock or wine, or even wrap them in bacon to ensure that they do not become dry.

LETTING THE ROAST REST
The cooking process doesn't end when you take a roast from the oven. Roasts need to rest, covered loosely with foil, for a few minutes or up to a half hour or more, depending on size, to allow the juices to be reabsorbed into the meat. As roasts rest, they continue to cook, which means that their internal temperature will rise, changing the degree of doneness. The larger the roast, the more the temperature increases. Good recipes will factor in this resting time to prevent overcooking.

PAN SAUCES AND DRIPPINGS

After many roasts have been cooked, there are brown bits and juices that remain in the pan. These drippings are loaded with flavor and can be used as the foundations for pan sauces. Simply remove the fat, add broth or wine to the pan, and heat to reduce the liquid and concentrate the flavors. A few swirls of butter will add body and shine to the sauce.

Pan sauces can also be thickened quickly with a paste made with equal amounts of softened butter and flour, referred to as *beurre manié* (French for "kneaded butter").

CARVING

For carving, I find that a wooden carving board with grooves around the sides for catching the juices is essential, as is a very sharp knife plus a carving fork for anchoring the roast. A chef's knife works well for beef, veal, lamb, and pork roasts, and for most poultry. For ham I like to use a long, slender, flexible knife. In some cases, kitchen shears work better; I use a pair for carving roast duck. For a large roasted fish fillet, use a sharp knife to cut it into servings, then a flat server or metal spatula to transfer to dinner plates.

For meat roasts, the thickness of the slice matters. The rule is that the more tender the cut, the thicker the slice can be. If a recipe does not specify how thick a slice should be, count on ¼ to ⅜ inch/6 mm to 9.5 mm as a good average size.

BEEF

From the Humble Pot Roast to a Glorious Standing Rib

There is nothing more enticing than the rich, complex smell of beef roasting in the oven. As a youngster, I remember listening to the crackle of fat as it slid from the meat into the roasting pan and knowing that dinner was at hand. Beef appeared on my family's table regularly since my dad worked as an administrator at a large meat company. Often he surprised my mother with a beautifully cut roast that she transformed into a feast for family and company alike.

When it comes to beef roasts, the choices are many. For special occasions, I frequently turn to high-end cuts—those glorious standing rib roasts and smooth-as-velvet tenderloins. Fortunately, there are more modestly priced possibilities, like short ribs, chuck roasts, and boneless top sirloins. With the proper preparation, they too will be juicy and succulent and burst with flavor. Regardless of which cut you select, look for quality and buy the best you can afford. For beef there are two primary grades—"prime" and "choice." The first is the best and most costly, and often reserved for restaurants.

"Choice" meats also make excellent roasts and are the ones most of us pick up in the market. Look also for marbling, those white flecks of fat that run throughout the meat. This internal fat will melt into your roast as it cooks, keeping it luscious and tender.

In the pages that follow, you will find some of my favorite recipes for beef roasts. On days when you want to prepare a homey, family meal, try the Old-Fashioned Pot Roast and Vegetables with Extra-Rich Pan Gravy or Roasted Beef Short Ribs in Barbecue Sauce. For holidays and celebrations, there are plenty of enticing entries, including Beef Tenderloin with Roasted Shallots, Bacon, and Port, New York Strip Loin with Béarnaise Butter and Smashed Fingerlings, and the festive Standing Rib Roast with Porcini Mushroom Sauce. And for Sunday roasting, why not savor the Perfect Sunday Roast? A richly browned sirloin served with a simple pan sauce, surrounded by roasted red onions and mushrooms, this mouthwatering dish will bring smiles to everyone at your table.

Old-Fashioned Pot Roast and Vegetables with Extra-Rich Pan Gravy

This is my idea of comfort food at its best. An inexpensive cut—a boneless chuck roast—is rubbed with crushed rosemary, basil, and red pepper flakes for extra flavor, then pan-seared. Next, the roast is slowly cooked in the oven in an aromatic mixture of beef broth, red wine, tomatoes, and root vegetables. Some of the fork-tender cooked vegetables are pureed and whisked into the pan liquids to thicken the delicious gravy.

Serves 5 to 6

COST: Inexpensive

PREP TIME: 45 minutes

START-TO-FINISH TIME:
3 hours, 45 minutes

1 boneless chuck roast, 3½ to 3¾ lb/
   1.6 to 1.7 kg
1 tbsp dried crushed rosemary
   (see cooking tip)
1½ tsp dried basil
Kosher salt
Freshly ground black pepper
½ tsp crushed red pepper flakes
3 tbsp olive oil
1½ cups/190 g halved and sliced onion
1 cup/140 g finely diced carrot
   (¼-in/6-mm cubes)
¾ cup/85 g finely diced celery
   (¼-in/6-mm cubes)
3 large garlic cloves, crushed and peeled
3 bay leaves, broken in half
One 28-oz/795-g can diced tomatoes, drained
3 cups/720 ml reduced-sodium beef broth
2 cups/480 ml dry red wine
½ cup/120 ml orange juice
2 tbsp minced flat-leaf parsley, for garnish

1. Arrange a rack at center position and preheat the oven to 350°F/180°C/gas 4.

2. Pat the roast dry with paper towels/absorbent paper. Combine rosemary, basil, 1 tsp salt, ½ tsp black pepper, and red pepper flakes in a small bowl and rub on all sides of the roast. In a deep-sided, ovenproof pot (with a lid) set over medium, heat 2 tbsp of the oil. When hot, add the meat and brown well on all sides, for about 5 minutes. Remove the roast and set aside.

3. In the same pot, heat the remaining 1 tbsp oil until hot over medium heat, and then add the onion, carrot, and celery. Cook, stirring, until the vegetables are softened, for 3 to 4 minutes. Add the garlic and sauté for 1 minute more. Add the bay leaves, tomatoes, broth, wine, and orange juice, and bring the mixture to a simmer. Return the meat to the pot; cover and roast in the oven until the meat is fork-tender, basting every 30 to 40 minutes with pan juices, about 2½ hours total.

4. Remove the roast to a serving platter and cover loosely with foil. Remove and discard the bay leaves. Skim off any fat and discard. With a slotted spoon, remove 1 cup/255 g of the vegetables in the pot and puree in a food processor or blender. Return the pureed vegetables to the pot, and place it over high heat. Reduce the liquids by a third. If not serving immediately, return the roast to the pot. (The roast can be prepared 2 days ahead; cool, cover, and refrigerate. Reheat, covered, in a 350°F/180°C/gas 4 preheated oven until the roast is heated through and the sauce is hot, for about 30 minutes.)

5. To serve, cut the roast into slices ¼ in/6 mm thick and serve topped with pan sauce and a sprinkle of parsley.

SIDES: Best-Ever Mashed Potatoes (page 138) and your favorite mixed greens salad tossed in red wine vinaigrette.

LEFTOVER TIP: Sliced leftover beef is delicious served atop a mound of buttered noodles with leftover sauce ladled over both.

COOKING TIP: If you can't find dried crushed rosemary, crush regular dried rosemary in an electric spice mill, or place it in a self-sealing plastic bag and roll over it with a rolling pin.

The Perfect Sunday Roast

Studded with garlic and seasoned with a simple rub, this boneless top sirloin roast is browned, and then placed in the oven along with a separate tray of red onion wedges and creminis. When served, the rosy pink beef slices are drizzled with a pan sauce, topped with thin slices of blue cheese, and surrounded with roasted vegetables. This roast needs only about an hour in the oven, and when done, both the tender meat and slightly charred vegetables boast a deep and richly satisfying flavor.

Serves 6 to 8

COST: Moderate

PREP TIME: 15 minutes for the roast, plus 15 minutes for the vegetables while the roast is in the oven

START-TO-FINISH TIME: 1 hour, 50 minutes, including resting time for cooked meat

One 4-lb/1.8-kg boneless top sirloin roast
   (see market note, page 22)
5 medium garlic cloves,
   peeled and cut into very thin slivers
2 tsp dried thyme leaves
Kosher salt
Freshly ground black pepper
3 tbsp plus ½ cup/120 ml olive oil,
   plus more for oiling the pans
3 medium red onions (about 1½ lb/680 g)
12 oz/340 g brown mushrooms such as
   creminis, cleaned and, if large, halved
1½ cups/360 ml reduced-sodium beef broth
¾ cup/180 ml dry red wine
1½ tbsp unsalted butter
1 bunch watercress
One 4-oz/115-g wedge of blue cheese

1. Pat the roast dry with paper towels/absorbent paper. Using a sharp paring knife, make slits over the entire surface of the roast and insert the garlic slivers. In a small bowl, mix together the thyme, 1½ tsp salt, ½ tsp pepper and 3 tbsp of the oil. Brush this mixture on all sides of the roast. (The roast can be prepared 1 day ahead; cover and refrigerate. Bring to room temperature for 30 minutes before proceeding.)

2. Arrange one rack at center position and another at a lower position and preheat the oven to 450°F/230°C/gas 8.

3. Lightly oil the bottom of a medium, flameproof roasting pan/tray and stand the roast, fat-side up, in the center of the pan (see cooking tip). Roast the meat for 15 minutes.

4. While the meat is roasting, prepare the onions and mushrooms. Oil a large, rimmed baking sheet/tray generously. Peel the onions and cut them into wedges ¾ in/2 cm thick, leaving the root ends intact. Arrange the onions on half of the baking sheet/tray and the mushrooms on the other half and drizzle both with the remaining ½ cup/120 ml olive oil. Toss the vegetables lightly to coat well, adding more oil if necessary. Salt and pepper the vegetables.

continued...

5. After the meat has roasted for 15 minutes, reduce the heat to 350°F/180°C/gas 4 and place the pan with the vegetables on the lower shelf. Continue to roast the beef until a thermometer inserted into the center of the meat registers 130 to 135°F/55 to 57°C, for 50 to 60 minutes. Roast the vegetables, stirring every 15 minutes, until slightly browned and charred around the edges, for 50 to 60 minutes.

6. When done, transfer the roast to a cutting board and let rest for 20 minutes. If the vegetables are not done when the roast is, continue roasting a few minutes more, checking every 5 minutes, until done. Remove the vegetables and tent them with foil to keep warm.

7. Skim off and discard any fat in the roasting pan/tray. Place the pan/tray over medium-high heat, and add the broth and wine. With a wire whisk, scrape up any browned bits on the bottom of the pan into the liquids. Bring the mixture to a simmer, and reduce by half. Then swirl in the butter. Season with salt and pepper.

8. Cut the roast, crosswise against the grain, into slices ¼ in/ 6 mm thick and arrange on a serving platter. Garnish the platter with bouquets of watercress and surround the meat with the onions and mushrooms. Drizzle the sliced meat with some sauce and pass extra separately. Top each serving with a thin slice of blue cheese.

SIDES: Pair this roast with Best-Ever Mashed Potatoes (page 138), or the Golden Potato Gratin (page 141), and with Green Beans with Caramelized Shallots (page 151)

LEFTOVER TIP: Sliced leftover beef is delicious used in sandwiches made with good peasant bread or a baguette. Slather some Dijon mustard on the bread, top with leftover roast beef, crumble any remaining blue cheese over, and add some watercress sprigs or a few arugula/ rocket or baby spinach leaves plus some sliced tomatoes.

MARKET NOTE: Ask your butcher for a roast cut from the top portion of the sirloin. These are more tender and sometimes referred to as "spoon roasts."

COOKING TIP: This particular cut of beef sometimes tips over as it roasts. To prevent this, you might want to use a roasting rack with sides that you can adjust to steady the meat.

Standing Rib Roast with Porcini Mushroom Sauce

This tall, stately roast with its rich marbled flesh is definitely meant for special occasions. Brushed with olive oil and seasoned with rosemary and coarse pepper, this big roast needs a long time in the oven, but when it comes out you'll be rewarded with exceptionally tender and flavorful meat. A glorious mushroom sauce, made with both dried porcini and fresh white mushrooms, can be partially prepared a day ahead and pairs exquisitely with the beef. For extra ease with carving, be sure to check the market note that follows the recipe.

Serves 8

COST: Splurge

PREP TIME: 35 minutes

START-TO-FINISH TIME: 4 hours, including resting time for cooked meat

1 standing rib roast with 4 ribs, about 8 to 9 lb/3.6 to 4 kg (see market note, page 25)

6½ tsp dried crushed rosemary (see cooking tip, page 19)

Kosher salt

Coarsely ground black pepper

½ cup/120 ml olive oil plus 2 tbsp

1½ oz dried porcini mushrooms

4 tbsp/55 g unsalted butter, at room temperature

10 oz/280 g white mushrooms, sliced ¼ in/6 mm thick

4 medium garlic cloves, minced

2 tbsp flour

1½ cups/360 ml reduced-sodium beef broth

¾ cup/180 ml dry red wine

2 bunches fresh rosemary for the garnish

1. Place the roast, fat-side up, in a heavy, shallow roasting pan/ tray. In a small bowl, mix together 4 tsp of the rosemary, 1 tbsp kosher salt, and 2 tsp pepper. Stir in the ½ cup/120 ml olive oil. Brush the roast on all sides, including the bottom, with this mixture. (The roast can be prepared 1 day ahead. Cover and refrigerate. Bring to room temperature for 45 minutes before roasting.)

2. Put the dried mushrooms in a medium bowl and cover with 2 cups/480 ml boiling water. Let stand until the mushrooms are softened, for 20 minutes. Strain the mushrooms in a fine strainer over a small bowl, pressing down on them to release as much liquid as possible. You should get 1 cup/ 240 ml; if not, add enough water to make this amount. Reserve the soaking liquid and coarsely chop the porcini.

3. Heat 2 tbsp of the butter and the remaining 2 tbsp olive oil in a large, heavy frying pan over medium-high heat. Add the white mushrooms and cook, stirring, until browned, for 5 to 6 minutes. Add the garlic and chopped porcini and cook, stirring, for 1 minute more. Season with ½ tsp kosher salt and several grinds of black pepper.

4. Combine the remaining 2 tbsp butter, remaining 2½ tsp rosemary, and flour in a small bowl and mash with a fork to make a paste. (The porcini soaking liquid, mushroom mix- ture, and butter-flour paste can be prepared 1 day ahead; cover separately and refrigerate.)

continued...

5. Arrange a rack at lower position and preheat the oven to 350°F/180°C/gas 4.

6. Roast until an instant-read meat thermometer inserted in the thickest part of the meat registers 125 to 130°F/52 to 55°C for meat that is rosy pink (medium-rare), for about 2 hours and 30 minutes.

7. Transfer the roast to a serving platter and cover loosely with foil. Let rest for 35 to 40 minutes while you prepare the sauce. Skim and discard any fat from the pan juices (there will be a small amount of pan drippings); reserve the juices in pan.

8. Set the roasting pan/tray over 2 burners on medium-high heat. Add the reserved porcini soaking liquid, the broth, and the wine. Bring to a boil, whisking constantly to scrape up any brown bits on the bottom and sides of the pan into the liquids, for about 2 to 3 minutes. Add the mushroom mixture and cook for 1 minute more. Whisk in the butter-flour mixture, a tablespoon at a time, and continue to whisk until the sauce thickens, for about 2 minutes. Season with salt and pepper.

9. To serve, garnish the roast on the platter with several bouquets of rosemary. Slice the roast and pass the mush-room sauce in a separate bowl.

SIDES: Yorkshire Pudding with Bacon and Sage (page 156) and Green Beans with Caramelized Shallots (page 151) are delectable accompaniments for this showstopper roast.

LEFTOVER TIP: What could be better than a warm roast beef open-faced sandwich made with succulent slices of this roast? Toast bread slices (a good sourdough is particularly nice), then top with slices of roast, and finally nap with leftover sauce.

MARKET NOTE: Ask the butcher to prepare an 8- to 9-lb/3.6- to 4-kg standing rib roast with 4 ribs. I usually request that the roast be "boned and tied." What this means is that the butcher removes the back or chine bone from the rack, then cuts the meat off in one piece from the ribs and finally ties it back on to the bones, so that the roast has the exact same appearance as one that has not been boned. At serving time, it's a breeze to slice the meat. The rib bones are still intact, but can be cut into individual servings for any guest who wants to nibble on one.

Pepper-Crusted Sirloin Roast with Horseradish Crème Fraîche

The same cut that is called for in the Perfect Sunday Roast (page 20) gets a totally new treatment in this version. The meat is coated with an assertive mixture of coarsely ground black pepper and butter, which helps baste the beef as it roasts. When done, the rosy pink, extra-juicy slices are topped with dollops of Horseradish Crème Fraîche. Its piquant flavor stands up well to the beef, and it has an unexpectedly light texture.

Serves 6 to 8

COST: Moderate

PREP TIME: 15 minutes

START-TO-FINISH TIME: 1 hour, 50 minutes, including resting time for cooked meat

Horseradish Crème Fraîche

½ cup/120 ml heavy/double cream

½ cup/120 ml crème fraîche (see cooking tip)

¼ cup/60 ml prepared horseradish (not horseradish sauce), drained, plus more if needed

3 tbsp minced shallots

2 tbsp capers, drained and coarsely chopped

2 tbsp minced fresh chives

1 tsp Dijon mustard

Kosher salt

Freshly ground black pepper

Roast

Vegetable oil, for greasing the roasting pan/tray

One 4-lb/1.8-kg boneless top sirloin roast (see market note)

Kosher salt

4 tbsp/55 g unsalted butter, at room temperature

2 large garlic cloves, minced

1 tbsp coarsely ground black pepper

FOR THE CRÈME FRAÎCHE:

With an electric mixer on medium-high speed, whip the heavy/double cream until stiff peaks form. In a medium, nonreactive bowl, whisk together the crème fraîche, horseradish, shallots, capers, 1½ tbsp of the chives, mustard, ¼ tsp salt, and ¼ tsp pepper. Gently fold in the whipped cream. Season with more salt and pepper if needed. Transfer to a small serving bowl and sprinkle with remaining chives. (Horseradish crème fraîche can be prepared 3 hours ahead; cover and refrigerate. Bring to room temperature for 10 minutes before serving.)

FOR THE ROAST:

1. Arrange a rack at center position and preheat the oven to 450°F/230°C/gas 8.

2. Lightly oil the bottom of a medium flameproof roasting pan/tray and stand the roast, fat-side up, in the center of the pan (see cooking tip). Sprinkle generously with salt. Combine the butter, garlic, pepper, and ¼ tsp salt in a small bowl and mix well. Pat the butter mixture over the top and partway down the rounded sides (not the big flat ends) of the roast.

3. Roast the meat for 15 minutes, then reduce the heat to 350°F/180°C/gas 4 and roast until a thermometer inserted into the center of the meat registers 130 to 135°F/55 to 57°C, for 50 to 60 minutes. When done, remove the roast to a cutting board; let rest for 20 minutes.

4. Cut the roast, crosswise against the grain, into slices ¼ in/ 6 mm thick and arrange on a serving platter. Garnish each slice with a generous dollop of crème fraîche before serving.

SIDES: Best-Ever Mashed Potatoes with Buttermilk–Country Mustard variation (page 138) and roasted or blanched asparagus are perfect sides for this roast.

LEFTOVER TIP: For tempting sandwiches, use a baguette or a crusty peasant loaf, top with sliced beef, spread with Horseradish Crème Fraîche, and then add some spinach or red leaf lettuce leaves.

MARKET NOTE: Ask your butcher for a roast cut from the top portion of the sirloin. These are more tender and sometimes referred to as "spoon roasts."

COOKING TIPS: Crème fraîche is available in many supermarkets, but if you can't find it, it's easy to prepare. Whisk together 1 cup/240 ml heavy/ double cream with ⅓ cup/75 ml sour cream in a nonreactive bowl, and let rest at room temperature for 6 hours or longer until mixture thickens. Cover and refrigerate for up to 5 days.

This particular cut of beef sometimes tips over as it roasts. To prevent this, you might want to use a roasting rack with sides that you can adjust to steady the meat.

New York Strip Loin with Béarnaise Butter and Smashed Fingerlings

What really makes this "meat-and-potatoes dish" special is the mouthwatering béarnaise butter that flavors both. A simple and quick version of classic béarnaise sauce, it is spooned atop the rosy-hued slices of strip loin and also incorporated into the warm fingerlings. Redolent of tarragon, this distinctive butter elevates both the roast and its potato garnish to new heights.

Serves 6

COST: Splurge

PREP TIME: 35 minutes, including making the butter

START-TO-FINISH TIME: 1 hour, 35 minutes, including resting time for cooked meat

Roast

1 New York strip loin roast,
  3 to 3½ lb/1.4 to 1.6 kg
  (also called a top loin; see market note)
Kosher salt
Freshly ground black pepper

Smashed Fingerlings

3 lb/1.4 kg red-skin fingerling or baby red-skin
  potatoes, unpeeled, scrubbed, cut into 1-in/
  2.5-cm pieces
Quick and Easy Béarnaise Butter (page 171)
½ cup/120 ml whole milk, warm, plus more
  if needed
Kosher salt
Freshly ground black pepper
1 tbsp minced flat-leaf parsley, for garnish
1 tbsp minced fresh tarragon, for garnish

FOR THE ROAST:

1. Arrange a rack at center position and preheat the oven to 450°F/230°C/gas 8.

2. Pat the beef dry with paper towels/absorbent paper. Salt and pepper the meat generously on all sides. Place the roast, fat-side up, on a rack in a large, heavy roasting pan/tray.

3. Roast the meat for 15 minutes, then reduce the heat to 350°F/180°C/gas 4, and roast until a thermometer inserted into the center of the meat registers 135°F/57°C, for about 30 minutes more. Remove from the oven and transfer to a carving board. Tent with foil and let rest for 15 to 20 minutes.

FOR THE SMASHED FINGERLINGS:

1. While the meat is in the oven, put the potatoes in a large pot and add enough water to cover them by 1 in/2.5 cm. Bring to a boil; cook until tender when pierced with a knife, for about 15 minutes. Drain and return the potatoes to the pot.

2. Add ½ cup/115 g of the béarnaise butter to the potatoes and smash coarsely with a potato masher. Add ½ cup/ 120 ml warm milk; stir to blend. Add more milk by table-spoons as needed if dry. Season with salt and pepper. (Potatoes can be prepared 2 hours ahead. Let rest at room temperature. Reheat before serving, adding more warm milk by tablespoonfuls as needed if dry.)

3. Slice the roast crosswise into slices ⅓ in/8 mm thick and arrange on a platter with a bowl of the remaining béarnaise butter by its side. Mound the potatoes in a serving bowl and sprinkle with parsley and tarragon. Serve each portion of sliced beef with a generous dollop of béarnaise butter and some potatoes.

SIDES: Either 5-Minute Roasted Sugar Snap Peas (page 149) or Honey-Glazed Carrots and Parsnips (page 145) would make a delicious garnish to the roast and smashed potatoes.

LEFTOVER TIP: For a great sandwich, slather any remaining béarnaise butter on a crusty baguette and top with any leftover sliced beef and some sliced tomatoes.

MARKET NOTE: A New York strip loin roast will have a layer of fat on one side; it is important to not trim this fat as it helps keep the meat moist while it roasts.

Rolled Flank Steak with a Corn Bread and Chorizo Stuffing

The testers for this book were crazy about this recipe, almost all commenting that they were thrilled to have a new way to prepare this popular cut. They were surprised to learn that you can easily butterfly, stuff, roll, and tie a flank steak so that it is transformed into a roast. For this version, a large flank steak is marinated in lime juice and olive oil, and then stuffed with a homemade corn bread filling studded with bits of chorizo, sweet orange bell peppers, and cilantro. When roasted and carved, the colorful corn bread layer makes an impressive visual counterpoint to the beautiful pink of the meat.

Serves 6

COST: Moderate

PREP TIME: 20 minutes for preparing the steak, plus 35 minutes for preparing the stuffing while the meat is marinating for 2 hours

START-TO-FINISH TIME: About 3 hours, including resting time for cooked meat

MATERIALS: Kitchen twine

Roast

One 1½-lb/690-g flank steak, about ¾ in/ 2 cm thick, butterflied (see market note)

⅓ cup/75 ml olive oil

2 tbsp fresh lime juice

½ tsp ground cumin

½ tsp kosher salt

¼ tsp red pepper flakes

Several grinds black pepper

2 medium garlic cloves, smashed

Stuffing

2 cups/110 g corn bread crumbs made from Quick Skillet Corn Bread (page 152)

1 tbsp olive oil

3 oz/85 g finely diced Spanish chorizo (see market note)

½ cup/65 g chopped onion

½ cup/65 g diced orange or red bell pepper/ capsicum

¼ cup/8 g minced cilantro/fresh coriander

½ tsp ground cumin

Kosher salt

Freshly ground black pepper

1 large egg, lightly beaten

FOR THE ROAST:

1. Place the butterflied flank steak on a long sheet of plastic wrap/cling film on a work surface. Cover with another sheet of plastic wrap/cling film, and pound with a meat pounder or rolling pin until the meat is about ¼ in/6 mm thick.

2. Whisk together the olive oil, lime juice, cumin, salt, red pepper flakes, and black pepper in a large, shallow non-reactive dish. Add the garlic cloves and then the flank steak, turning to coat well. Cover with plastic wrap/cling film and refrigerate for 2 hours or longer.

FOR THE STUFFING:

1. Put the corn bread crumbs in a large mixing bowl. Heat the olive oil in a medium, heavy frying pan over medium heat. When hot, add the chorizo, onion, and bell pepper/ capsicum. Stir and cook until chorizo is lightly browned and vegetables are softened, for about 5 minutes. Add to the corn bread crumbs and mix well. Stir in the cilantro/ fresh coriander and cumin; season with salt and pepper. Cool completely, and then mix in the egg.

2. Remove the flank steak from the marinade, scraping off any excess, and place it on a work surface. Reserve the marinade, discarding the garlic. Salt and pepper the steak, then pat the stuffing very compactly in an even layer on the steak, leaving a 1-in/2.5-cm border all around. With a long side in front of you, roll the meat tightly into a cylinder and tie at 1-in/2.5-cm intervals. (The flank steak can be prepared 4 hours ahead; cover and refrigerate. Refrigerate the marinade separately. Bring both to room temperature for 30 minutes before roasting.)

3. Arrange a rack at center position and preheat the oven to 350°F/180°C/gas 4.

4. Place the flank steak in a shallow roasting pan/tray, and pour the reserved marinade over it. Roast for 30 minutes, basting twice with pan juices, or until the center of the meat is rosy pink when pierced with a small sharp knife. Remove and tent loosely with foil and let rest for 15 minutes. Cut into slices ½ in/12 mm thick and serve.

SIDES: Corn on the cob and a sliced tomato and avocado salad would make tempting sides to this special roast with its assertive Southwestern flavors.

LEFTOVER TIP: Slices of this flank steak are delicious served at room temperature. Add a green salad tossed in lime juice and olive oil for a light lunch or supper.

MARKET NOTES: When you buy the flank steak, use your most persuasive and polite voice to ask the butcher to butterfly it for you. If you butterfly it yourself, use a long, sharp knife and starting at a long side, cut the meat horizontally, almost but not quite all the way through, so it will open like a book.

Chorizo is a highly seasoned pork sausage available in both Spanish and Mexican varieties. For this recipe, use the firmer Spanish type, which is made with smoked pork that is already cooked, not the Mexican one, which is prepared with fresh pork enclosed in a casing.

Beef Tenderloin with Roasted Shallots, Bacon, and Port

It's the tantalizing sauce, layered with multiple flavors, that makes this roast so distinctive. Sweet, caramelized shallots and salty bits of bacon are added to a reduction of port and broth to form its foundation. At serving time, juicy slices of tenderloin are napped with this smooth, silky mixture.

Serves 6

COST: Splurge

PREP TIME: 40 minutes

START-TO-FINISH TIME: 2 hours, including resting time for cooked meat

12 oz/340 g (about 12) large shallots, peeled and halved lengthwise

1½ tbsp olive oil

Kosher salt

Freshly ground black pepper

3 cups/720 ml reduced-sodium beef broth

¾ cup/180 ml Tawny port (see market note)

1½ tsp tomato paste/puree

One 3-lb/1.4-kg trimmed center cut beef tenderloin

1 tsp dried thyme

4 bacon/streaky bacon slices (about 4 oz/ 115 g), coarsely chopped

3 tbsp unsalted butter, at room temperature

½ tbsp flour

1 bunch watercress

1. Arrange a rack at center position and preheat the oven to 375°F/190°C/gas 5.

2. In a medium roasting pan/tray (a 9-in/23-cm pie plate will also work), toss the shallots with the oil to coat, and season with salt and pepper. Roast until the shallots are deep brown and very tender, stirring occasionally, for 30 to 40 minutes or longer. Remove, but retain oven temperature.

3. Boil the broth and the port in a medium saucepan until reduced to about 1½ cups/360 ml, for 20 to 25 minutes. Whisk in the tomato paste/puree. (Both shallots and broth mixture can be prepared 1 day ahead. Cover separately and refrigerate.)

4. Pat the beef dry and sprinkle with thyme, salt, and pepper. In a medium roasting pan/tray set over medium heat, sauté the bacon until golden, for 4 minutes or more, then transfer it with a slotted spoon to paper towels/absorbent paper to drain. Increase the heat to medium-high and add the tenderloin to the pan. Brown well on all sides, for about 7 minutes. Transfer the pan to the oven and roast until a meat thermometer inserted into the thickest part of the roast reads 135°F/57°C for medium-rare, for about 45 minutes. Transfer the meat to a platter and tent loosely with foil. Let rest for 15 to 20 minutes.

5. Skim and discard any fat from the pan juices, then set the roasting pan/tray over high heat. Add the broth-port mixture and bring to a boil, scraping up the browned bits on the bottom of the pan. Mix ½ tbsp of the butter and the flour in a small bowl to make a smooth paste. Whisk the paste into the simmering liquids and simmer the sauce until slightly thickened, for 3 to 4 minutes.

6. Whisk the remaining butter into the sauce, and then stir in the shallots and bacon. Season the sauce with salt and pepper.

7. Cut the tenderloin into slices ½ in/12 mm thick and arrange on a platter. Spoon some sauce over the slices and put the remaining sauce in a small bowl to pass. Garnish the platter with watercress and serve.

SIDES: Spoon some of the delectable sauce over Best-Ever Mashed Potatoes (page 138) and complete the offerings with Honey-Glazed Carrots and Parsnips (page 145).

LEFTOVER TIP: A warm open-faced sandwich made with slices of this special roast would be a real treat. Toast bread slices (a good sourdough is particularly nice), then top with thin slices of roast, and finally nap with leftover sauce.

MARKET NOTE: There are four types of port: Vintage, Tawny, Ruby, and White. You don't need to use the most expensive, which is the Vintage. The ready-to-drink Tawny, which is the same color as its name, is a good moderately priced choice, but if it is not available, you can use a less expensive Ruby port.

Beef Tenderloin Stuffed with Spinach, Mascarpone, and Sun-Dried Tomatoes

This recipe is an unusual yet impressive way to prepare a beef tenderloin. The meat is butterflied and pounded to an even thickness, then topped with a Mediterranean melange of sun-dried tomatoes, spinach, creamy mascarpone, and grated Parmesan. Rolled tightly into a cylinder and tied, the tenderloin is roasted, and then carved into slices that reveal an interesting pattern of colors.

Serves 6

COST: Splurge

PREP TIME: 30 minutes

START-TO-FINISH TIME: 1 hour, 40 minutes, including resting time for cooked meat

MATERIALS: Kitchen twine

1¼ lb/550 g spinach, stemmed and cleaned (not baby spinach)

8 oz/225 g mascarpone

¼ cup/30 g grated Parmesan cheese, preferably Parmigiano-Reggiano

½ tsp dried crushed rosemary (see cooking tip, page 19)

½ tsp dried thyme leaves

Kosher salt

Freshly ground black pepper

One 2½-lb/1.2-kg trimmed center cut beef tenderloin (see market note, page 36)

½ cup/115 g drained oil-packed sun-dried tomatoes, chopped

3 tbsp olive oil

1 tbsp minced flat-leaf parsley (optional)

1. Set aside 10 to 12 large spinach leaves. Blanch the remaining spinach in boiling water to cover until just wilted, for 1 to 2 minutes. Place the spinach in a strainer and run under cold water to cool. Drain well, then place in a clean kitchen towel; squeeze and wring out all excess water. Chop the spinach coarsely.

2. In a medium bowl, mix together the mascarpone and Parmesan, then add the cooked spinach, rosemary, thyme, ½ tsp salt, and ¼ tsp pepper. Mix until well blended.

3. Make a slit lengthwise down the center of the tenderloin, cutting two-thirds of the way through the meat. Spread the meat open and pound with a meat pounder until it is ½ in/12 mm thick. Season with salt and pepper.

4. Lay the reserved spinach leaves over the meat in an overlapping layer, leaving a 1-in/2.5-cm border all around. Next, spread the sun-dried tomatoes over the spinach leaves. Shape the spinach-mascarpone mixture into a log the same length as the meat and center it over the tomatoes. Starting at a long edge, roll the tenderloin as tightly as possible into a cylinder, enclosing the spinach-mascarpone log as you roll. Tie the meat tightly at 1-in/2.5-cm intervals. If any of the spinach filling starts to ooze out at the ends, remove it and save for another use (such as the filling for an omelet). (The tenderloin can be prepared 4 hours ahead; cover and refrigerate. Bring to room temperature 30 minutes before roasting.)

continued…

5. Arrange a rack at center position and preheat the oven to 375°F/190°C/gas 5.

6. Heat the oil in a medium, flameproof roasting pan/tray set over medium-high heat. When the oil is very hot, add the tenderloin and brown well on all sides, for 5 minutes. Salt and pepper the meat generously. Place the pan/tray in the oven and roast until a thermometer inserted into the center of the meat registers 135 to 140°F/57 to 60°C for medium-rare, for about 25 minutes. You can also check for doneness by making a slit in the center of the meat to check its color. It should be very pink when ready to come out of the oven.

7. Transfer the meat to a platter and tent loosely with foil. Let rest for 15 to 20 minutes. Remove the strings and cut the tenderloin into slices ½ in/12 mm thick and arrange on a platter. Sprinkle with some parsley, if desired, and serve.

SIDES: Golden Potato Gratin (page 141) and blanched tender green beans sprinkled with sea salt would make excellent garnishes. If you want to be more adventurous, replace the green beans with broccoli rabe, the bitter Italian green. Blanch, then sauté the stalks in olive oil along with garlic, pine nuts, and raisins.

LEFTOVER TIP: For a simple lunch or supper, serve leftover slices at room temperature with a green salad dressed with lemon juice and olive oil.

MARKET NOTE: When buying the tenderloin for this recipe, it's important that you ask for a center cut. You want the diameter of the roast to be the same throughout and not tapered at one end, if possible.

Mini Wellingtons

One of the most celebrated roasts of all time, classic beef Wellington is an elaborate preparation in which a tenderloin is topped with foie gras and mushroom duxelles, then encased in puff pastry and baked. The catch is to make certain that the meat and the pastry cook to the correct doneness at exactly the same time. In my updated version, I use individual tenderloin steaks instead of a whole roast, and replace the foie gras and mushrooms with caramelized shallots, grated Gruyère, and a generous dollop of whole-grain Dijon mustard. The petite steaks with their new adornments are wrapped in squares of purchased puff pastry and can be readied several hours ahead. At roasting time, you'll discover as I did that both the meat and the pastry cook to perfection in only a few minutes!

Serves 4

COST: Splurge

PREP TIME: 55 minutes including sautéing the shallots and assembling the steaks in puff pastry

START-TO-FINISH TIME: 2 hours, including chilling and resting time for cooked meat

½ lb/225 g shallots, peeled and
    halved lengthwise
1½ tbsp unsalted butter
3½ tbsp olive oil
Kosher salt
Freshly ground black pepper
Four 1-in/2.5-cm-thick beef tenderloin steaks,
    4½ oz/130 g each (see market note, page 39)
About 5 tsp whole-grain Dijon mustard
¼ cup/20 g grated Gruyère cheese
Flour for rolling out the pastry
1 sheet puff pastry from a 17.3-oz/
    490-g package, defrosted
1 beaten egg
Canola or olive oil for the baking sheet/tray
Fleur de sel or Maldon salt (see market note,
    page 39)

1. Cut the halved shallots crosswise into slices ½ in/12 mm thick. Melt the butter and 1½ tbsp of the oil in a large, heavy frying pan over medium heat. When hot, add the shallots and reduce the heat to medium-low. Cook, stirring frequently, until the shallots are nicely browned, translucent, and tender, for 12 minutes or longer.

2. Salt and pepper the steaks on one side. Heat a heavy, medium frying pan for 3 to 4 minutes over high heat until the pan is very hot. Add the remaining 2 tbsp oil and, when hot, sear the steaks for just 1 minute per side. Remove the steaks to a dinner plate and let cool for 5 minutes. Top each steak with a generous teaspoon of mustard, one-quarter of the shallots, and 1 tbsp of the cheese.

3. On a floured work surface, roll the puff pastry into a 12-in/30.5-cm square and cut it into 4 squares. Brush a ½-in/12-mm border around each square with the beaten egg, and refrigerate the remaining beaten egg.

continued...

4. Place a pastry square (brushed-side down) over a steak; carefully lift up the meat and press the pastry around its sides, then seal tightly on the bottom. Place on a lightly oiled baking sheet/tray, and repeat with remaining steaks. Refrigerate the Mini Wellingtons for 45 minutes to 1 hour.

5. Arrange a rack at center position and preheat the oven to 425°F/220°C/gas 7.

6. Brush the top and sides (but not the bottoms) of the pastry enclosing each steak with some of the reserved beaten egg and sprinkle the tops with a pinch of fleur de sel.

7. Roast the Mini Wellingtons until the pastry is golden brown and a thermometer inserted through the pastry into the center of the meat registers 135 to 140°F/57 to 60°C for medium-rare, for 15 to 18 minutes.

8. Transfer the Mini Wellingtons to a rack and let rest for 5 minutes before serving.

SIDES: These Mini Wellingtons are rich so you might want to offer simple garnishes. Try them with asparagus seasoned with butter and a sprinkle of sea salt and with a watercress salad dressed in red wine vinaigrette.

LEFTOVER TIP: It's unlikely you'll have any Mini Wellingtons left over, but if so, they make great cold sandwiches.

MARKET NOTES: For this recipe, try to buy tenderloin steaks that are as close in size and weight as possible so that they will roast at the same time. Steaks that are 1 in/2.5 cm thick and about 4½ oz/130 g work best.

Fleur de sel (which translates as "flower of salt") is a French sea salt that is harvested by hand. Known for its rich taste of trace minerals, it is a great flavor booster and is often sprinkled on finished dishes as a final seasoning.
  Maldon salt is an English sea salt with large crystals and a robust flavor.
  Both fleur de sel and Maldon salt are available in specialty food stores and in some supermarkets.

Roasted Beef Short Ribs in Barbecue Sauce

If you've never roasted short ribs, you're in for a treat. This inexpensive cut takes to slow oven cooking naturally, with mouthwatering results. In the following recipe, these ribs are rubbed with an earthy blend of brown sugar, smoked paprika, and other robust spices, then browned and simmered in a barbecue sauce, which conveniently cooks along with them. When done, the short ribs are fork-tender and bursting with smoky, sweet, and tart flavors. An added bonus is that these ribs improve in flavor when made in advance and reheated.

Serves 6

COST: Inexpensive

PREP TIME: 30 minutes for prepping the ribs and barbecue sauce

START-TO-FINISH TIME: 2 hours, 30 minutes, plus 6 hours or overnight to marinate the ribs

Ribs
4½ lb/2 kg beef short ribs
  (10 to 12 ribs, depending on the size)
1½ tbsp light brown sugar
1 tbsp ground cumin
1 tbsp smoked paprika (see market note)
1½ tsp kosher salt
1½ tsp freshly ground black pepper
½ tsp cayenne pepper
¼ tsp ground cinnamon

Quick Pan Barbecue Sauce
1½ cups/420 g ketchup/tomato sauce
1 cup/200 g light brown sugar
½ cup/120 ml red wine vinegar
¼ cup/60 ml Worcestershire sauce
2½ tbsp dry mustard/mustard powder,
  such as Coleman's
2 tsp smoked paprika
2 tsp hot sauce
1½ tsp kosher salt
1½ tsp freshly ground black pepper

Olive oil for sautéing
2 tbsp minced flat-leaf parsley, for garnish
  (optional)

FOR THE RIBS:
1. Pat the ribs dry with paper towels/absorbent paper. Mix the brown sugar, cumin, paprika, salt, pepper, cayenne, and cinnamon in a small bowl and rub on all sides of the ribs. Place the ribs on a large plate, cover with plastic wrap/cling film, and refrigerate for 6 hours or overnight.

2. Arrange a rack at center position and preheat the oven to 350°F/180°C/gas 4.

FOR THE SAUCE:
1. Use a large, heavy, flameproof roasting pan/tray that will hold the ribs comfortably in a single layer. Add ketchup/tomato sauce, brown sugar, vinegar, Worcestershire sauce, mustard, paprika, hot sauce, salt, pepper, and ½ cup/120 ml water to the pan and whisk until well blended.

2. Coat a large, heavy frying pan lightly with olive oil and place over medium heat. When hot, sear the ribs on all sides until lightly browned, watching carefully so that their coating does not burn. Place the ribs in the roasting pan/tray and turn to coat well with sauce. Place the pan over 1 to 2 burners on high heat and bring the mixture to a bubbling simmer. Remove and cover the pan tightly with a double thickness of foil. Roast until the ribs are fork-tender, for 1½ to 2 hours or longer.

3. Remove the ribs from the oven and skim off and discard all the fat (there will be a lot) from the pan. (Ribs can be prepared 1 day ahead; cool them and the sauce to room temperature, but do not skim off fat if making in advance. Remove the ribs to a separate container. Cover and refrigerate the ribs and the sauce separately. When chilled, the fat in the sauce will congeal and can be removed and discarded easily. To reheat, return the ribs to the pan with the sauce, cover with foil, and place in a 350°F/180°C/gas 4 preheated oven until hot, for 20 to 30 minutes.)

4. Serve the ribs coated with some sauce and sprinkled with parsley, if desired. Pass any extra sauce in a bowl.

SIDES: Best-Ever Mashed Potatoes Blue Cheese variation (page 138) and a green salad would make tempting accompaniments.

LEFTOVER TIP: These short ribs freeze very well so you can save any leftovers for up to 1 month.

MARKET NOTE: Spanish smoked paprika, called pimenton, is available in gourmet food stores and in some groceries, or you can order it online from Penzeys at www.penzeys.com. I used the sweet (dulce) style.

PORK

Popular, Plentiful, and Versatile

As a young, fledging cook, I often turned to my Southern family's recipes for inspiration, but when it came to pork, I had to look elsewhere. The simple fact is that today's pork is quite different from the meat that was available to an older generation of cooks.

First, it is bred to be leaner, and this requires some significant adaptations to ensure a moist, succulent roast. In the recipes that follow you will be urged to baste frequently so that the meat does not dry out. Second, today's pork does not need to be cooked to those high internal temperatures of 170 to 180°F/77 to 82°C that used to be recommended for safety reasons. Most professional cooks agree that 150°F/65°C is perfect—the point at which pork roasts retain a slight blush of pink and are moist and flavorful.

This chapter reflects a breadth of choices when it comes to pork. From inexpensive shoulders and hams to premium tenderloins and racks, there are a variety of cuts that are suited for roasting and readily available at meat counters. One of pork's outstanding features is its versatility. You can pair it with fruits, herbs, spices, cheeses, and much more, so you will find some imaginative creations in this section. Pork Loin with a Blue Cheese Stuffing and Roasted Pears, Ham with an Orange Marmalade Glaze and Rhubarb Chutney, and Cumin-Rubbed Pork Tenderloins with Fresh Peach Salsa should whet your appetite. For showstopper entrees you can't beat the glorious Crown Roast of Pork with Tarragon-Mustard Butter or the impressive Racks of Pork with Apple Chutney.

Pork Tenderloins with Cranberry–Port Wine Sauce

This is a splendid main course for special occasions. A platter with succulent slices of roasted pork tenderloin, napped with crimson-hued cranberry port sauce, makes a striking centerpiece for a holiday meal. The sauce can be cooked and the tenderloins seasoned with the herb rub a day ahead, so that all you'll need to do before serving is to roast the pork for about 20 minutes.

Serves 8

COST: Moderate

PREP TIME: 45 minutes, including making the sauce

START-TO-FINISH TIME: 1 hour, 30 minutes, including resting time for the cooked meat

Cranberry–Port Wine Sauce
3 tbsp unsalted butter

2 cups/250 g chopped onions

4 medium garlic cloves, minced

3 tsp grated orange zest

1½ tsp dried sage leaves

1 tsp dried thyme

2 cups/480 ml reduced-sodium chicken broth

1½ cups/360 ml cranberry juice cocktail (see market note)

2 cups (8 oz/225 g) fresh or frozen (defrosted) cranberries

½ cup/100 g sugar

¼ cup/60 ml Tawny port (see market note, page 33)

1 tbsp cornstarch/cornflour

Kosher salt

Freshly ground black pepper

Pork
4½ tsp dried thyme

1½ tsp kosher salt

1½ tsp freshly ground black pepper

Three 1-lb/455-g pork tenderloins, trimmed of excess fat

4 tbsp/60 ml vegetable oil

FOR THE WINE SAUCE:

1. In a large, heavy frying pan set over medium-high heat, melt the butter and, when hot, add the onions. Sauté, stirring, until golden and softened, about 8 minutes. Add the garlic, half of the orange zest, sage, and thyme and stir 1 minute. Add the broth and cranberry juice and simmer until the mixture has reduced to 2½ cups/600 ml, for about 8 minutes.

2. Strain the sauce into a heavy, medium saucepan, pressing down on the solids with the back of a spoon to extract as much liquid as possible; discard the solids. Place the saucepan over medium heat and stir in the cranberries and sugar. Bring to a boil and cook just until the cranberries pop, for about 5 minutes.

3. In a small bowl, whisk together the port and cornstarch/cornflour to form a paste. Add to the sauce and stir until the sauce thickens, for 1 minute. Season with salt and pepper. (Cranberry port sauce can be prepared 1 day ahead; cool, cover, and refrigerate.)

FOR THE PORK:

1. Mix together the thyme, salt, and pepper in a small bowl. Pat the tenderloins dry with paper towels/absorbent paper, then brush them with 2 tbsp of the oil. Rub the herb mixture over the tenderloins. (The pork can be prepared 1 day ahead; cover and refrigerate.)

2. Arrange a rack at center position and preheat the oven to 400°F/200°C/gas 6.

3. Heat the remaining oil in a large, heavy, flameproof roasting pan/tray set over 1 to 2 burners on high heat. When the oil is hot, add the tenderloins and brown on all sides, for 5 minutes. Roast the pork until an instant-read thermometer inserted into the thickest part registers 150°F/65°C, for about 20 minutes. Transfer the pork to a carving board, tent with foil, and let rest for 10 minutes.

4. Skim off and discard any fat in the roasting pan/tray. Add the wine sauce and the remaining orange zest and set the pan/tray over 1 to 2 burners on high heat and bring to a simmer, stirring frequently.

5. To serve, cut the pork into diagonal slices ½ in/12 mm thick and drizzle with some sauce. Pass extra sauce separately.

SIDES: Serve this roast with some creamy polenta seasoned with grated Gruyère cheese and Brussels sprouts sautéed with garlic. For a holiday menu, offer the Wild Rice with Roasted Grapes and Walnuts (page 155) and tender green beans.

LEFTOVER TIP: Slices of this tenderloin are delicious simply warmed up with some of the sauce. You could also use the pork in a sandwich. Use sourdough bread slices or a crusty baguette and top with leftover pork, sliced white cheddar, and some of the sauce, brought to room temperature.

MARKET NOTE: Cranberry juice cocktail is available in the juice aisle of the supermarket.

Cumin-Rubbed Pork Tenderloins with Fresh Peach Salsa

When temperatures soar and you are looking for a quick, easy, and cooling main course, these tenderloins are the answer. The pork needs only about 20 minutes in the oven, and the colorful, bracing salsa can be assembled in just a few minutes.

Serves 4 to 5

COST: Moderate

PREP TIME: 25 minutes, including making the salsa

START-TO-FINISH TIME: 1 hour, including resting time for cooked meat

2 tsp ground cumin

1 tsp kosher salt

1 tsp freshly ground black pepper

2 pork tenderloins, about 1 lb/455 g each, trimmed of excess fat

Olive oil for sautéing

Fleur de sel (optional)

Fresh Peach Salsa (page 169)

1. Arrange a rack at center position and preheat the oven to 400°F/200°C/gas 6.

2. In a small bowl, mix together the cumin, salt, and pepper. Rub this mixture over all the surfaces of the tenderloins. Add enough oil to coat the bottom of a large, heavy, oven-proof frying pan and set it over medium-high heat until the oil is hot. Add the tenderloins and brown on all sides, for 5 minutes.

3. Roast the pork until a thermometer inserted into the thickest part of the meat registers 150°F/65°C, for about 20 minutes. Remove the tenderloins to a carving board and let rest for 10 minutes.

4. To serve, slice the pork ½-in/12-mm thick and arrange, slightly overlapping, on a platter. If desired, sprinkle the slices lightly with fleur de sel. Spoon some peach salsa over the slices and pass any extra salsa in a bowl.

SIDES: Couscous tossed with butter and minced chives and 5-Minute Roasted Sugar Snap Peas (page 149) would make ideal sides to this main course.

LEFTOVER TIP: Slices of this pork are just as good served cold as warm, especially when accompanied by some of the peach salsa. For a great sandwich, spread some mayo on lightly toasted whole-wheat bread, top with pork, then with salsa, and finally with a few baby spinach leaves.

Pork Loin with a Blue Cheese Stuffing and Roasted Pears

Natural partners, blue cheese and pears can be used inventively to turn an ordinary pork loin into something extra-special. The cheese finds its way into the herbed bread stuffing, which is packed compactly into the center of this boneless roast. Quartered pears, brushed with a balsamic glaze, roast alongside the meat. The pork slices with their delicious nuggets of stuffing are napped with a simple pan sauce and garnished with golden pear wedges.

Serves 6

COST: Moderate

PREP TIME: 30 minutes, including making the fresh bread crumbs

START-TO-FINISH TIME: 1 hour, 40 minutes, including resting time for cooked meat

One 2½-lb/1.2-kg center-cut boneless pork loin, trimmed and tied

2 tbsp dried crushed rosemary (see cooking tip, page 19)

2 tbsp dried thyme leaves

1 tsp kosher salt

1 tsp freshly ground black pepper

1½ cups/85 g fresh bread crumbs (see cooking tip, page 48)

1 cup/115 g crumbled blue cheese

3 tbsp plus 1 cup/240 ml reduced-sodium chicken broth

4 to 5 tbsp/60 to 75 ml olive oil

3 tbsp balsamic vinegar

3 slightly under-ripe Bartlett/Williams or Bosc pears, unpeeled, quartered, and cored (keep stems on the pears if you like)

2 tbsp unsalted butter

Fresh rosemary and thyme sprigs, for garnish (optional)

1. Using a long, narrow knife, insert the blade into the center of one end the pork and push the knife all the way through to the other end. Turn the knife to create a pocket about 1 in/2.5 cm in diameter all the way through the roast.

2. Mix together the rosemary, thyme, salt, and pepper. Put half of this mixture in a bowl with the bread crumbs and the cheese; reserve the rest.

3. Using your fingers, rub together the bread crumb mixture (as you would for a crumble), and then stir in 2½ to 3 tbsp of the broth, just enough to moisten mixture. Using the end of a wooden spoon (or, if easier, your thumb), push the stuffing into the pocket to within ½ in/12 mm of each end. (It will seem as if you have too much stuffing, but it will be compacted as it is pushed into the cavity.) Pat the roast dry with paper towels/absorbent paper and rub the remaining seasoning mixture over the entire surface. (The roast can be prepared 4 hours ahead; cover and refrigerate.)

4. Arrange a rack at center position and preheat the oven to 400°F/200°C/gas 6.

5. In a medium bowl, whisk together 2 tbsp of the olive oil and 2 tbsp of the balsamic vinegar, then add the pears and toss to coat.

continued...

6. In a large, flameproof roasting pan/tray, add the remaining 2 tbsp oil, or enough to lightly cover the bottom, and set the pan over 1 to 2 burners on medium-high heat. When the oil is hot, brown the pork on all sides, for 6 to 8 minutes. Place the pan in the oven and roast the pork for 10 minutes, and then scatter the pears, skin-sides up, around the meat. Roast for another 10 minutes, and then turn the meat and pears. Continue roasting until an instant-read thermometer registers 150°F/65°C when inserted into the thickest part of the meat and the pears are tender and golden, for 20 to 25 minutes longer. Remove the meat and pears to a cutting board; cover loosely with foil and let rest for 15 minutes. Remove and discard (or sample!) any loose stuffing from the pan. Skim off and discard any fat in the pan.

7. Place the roasting pan/tray over high heat and add the remaining 1 cup/240 ml broth and remaining 1 tbsp vinegar; reduce the liquids by a third while scraping the bits on the bottom of the pan into the sauce. Swirl in the butter and season with additional salt if needed.

8. To serve, slice the roast ¾ in/2 cm thick, removing the strings. Place the slices on a serving platter and garnish with the pears and, if desired, with fresh herbs. Drizzle the meat and pears with some pan sauce.

SIDES: Honey-Glazed Carrots and Parsnips (page 145) would make a colorful and tempting accompaniment for this roast.

LEFTOVER TIP: Serve leftover slices as you would a pâté or terrine with some French cornichons and a good crusty baguette. A green salad tossed in a vinaigrette could round out the garnishes.

COOKING TIP: To make coarse bread crumbs, use a good-quality peasant or country bread loaf that is 1 to 2 days old; sourdough works particularly well. Remove the crust and process large chunks of the bread in a food processor until you have 1½ cups.

Orange-Scented Pork Roast with Fennel and Potatoes

This boneless pork loin roast bursts with vibrant flavors, is not complicated to prepare, and needs less than an hour in the oven. Studded with garlic slivers, quickly browned, then brushed with a glaze made with balsamic vinegar, orange marmalade, and mustard, the meat is roasted along with fennel and potato wedges. When done, the pork has a deep mahogany hue and the vegetables are slightly crisp and golden around the edges. A quick sauce is assembled using the pan juices and some additional glaze.

Serves 6

COST: Moderate

PREP TIME: 35 minutes

START-TO-FINISH TIME: 1 hour, 30 minutes, including resting time for cooked meat

One 2½-lb/1.2-kg center cut boneless pork loin, trimmed and tied

3 large garlic cloves, peeled and cut into thin slivers

3 medium fennel bulbs (about 2 lb/910 g total)

1 lb/455 g small Yukon gold potatoes, scrubbed but not peeled

4 tbsp/60 ml olive oil

Kosher salt

Freshly ground black pepper

2 tbsp balsamic vinegar

3 tbsp orange marmalade

1 tbsp fresh orange juice

1 tsp Dijon mustard

2 tbsp unsalted butter

1½ tbsp minced flat-leaf parsley, for garnish

Thin orange slices, for garnish (optional)

1. Arrange a rack at center position and preheat the oven to 400°F/200°C/gas 6.

2. Using a sharp paring knife, make slits over the entire surface of the pork and insert the garlic slivers.

3. Cut off and discard the lacy stems from the fennel bulbs. Cut and discard a slice from the bases, then halve the bulbs lengthwise and cut out and discard the tough triangular cores in each half. Slice each half lengthwise into ½-in-/12-mm-thick wedges. Cut the potatoes in half lengthwise and then cut lengthwise into ½-in-/12-mm-thick wedges. Place a large, flameproof roasting pan/tray over 1 or 2 burners on medium-high heat and add 2 tbsp of the oil. When hot, add the fennel and potatoes and sauté, stirring, to soften just slightly, for about 5 minutes. Remove the vegetables and set aside.

4. Heat the remaining 2 tbsp of oil in the roasting pan/tray until hot. Add the pork and brown well on all sides, for 6 to 8 minutes. Scatter the vegetables evenly around the roast and generously salt and pepper the roast and vegetables.

5. In a bowl, whisk together the vinegar, marmalade, orange juice, and mustard. Remove 2 to 3 tbsp of this mixture and brush it on the top and sides of the roast.

6. Roast until a meat thermometer inserted into the thickest part of the meat reads 150°F/65°C and the vegetables are browned and tender, for 40 to 45 minutes or longer. Stir the vegetables every 10 minutes while roasting.

7. Remove the pork to a carving board and the vegetables to a platter. Brush the meat with 1 to 2 tsp of the glaze. Tent the meat and the vegetables with foil; let rest for 15 minutes.

8. For the sauce, skim and discard any fat in the roasting pan/ tray. Then add the butter and remaining glaze mixture to the pan/tray. Place the pan/tray over medium-high heat and bring the mixture a simmer. Cook until slightly thickened, for 2 to 3 minutes.

9. To serve, slice the pork and arrange on a platter surrounded by the potatoes and fennel. Sprinkle both with parsley. If desired, garnish the pork with some orange slices.

SIDES: Since this pork is roasted with potatoes and fennel, you will not have to worry about accompaniments.

LEFTOVER TIP: Stir-fry thinly sliced strips of leftover pork with sliced vegetables and season them with minced ginger and soy sauce.

Crown Roast of Pork with Tarragon-Mustard Butter

What could be more impressive than a crown roast of pork when you want an extra-special main course for a crowd? Although you might think that this roast, which serves 16, requires advanced culinary skills, it's actually uncomplicated to prepare. Two tips will ensure success. First, this roast is always a special order so it's helpful to understand that the butcher will be tying two racks of pork together to form a crown when he or she prepares it. Second, because this roast spends a long time in the oven, the meat needs to be basted often with the seasoned butter to keep it moist. Follow these two guidelines, and you'll bring a show stopping roast to the table!

Serves 16, with one chop each

COST: Moderate

PREP TIME: 20 minutes, including making the butter

START-TO-FINISH TIME: 2 hours, 45 minutes, to 3 hours, 15 minutes, including resting time for cooked meat

A double recipe of Tarragon-Mustard Butter (page 172)

1 crown roast of pork with 16 ribs, about 8 lb/3.6 kg total (see market note)

4 large garlic cloves, peeled and cut into thin slivers

⅓ cup/75 ml crème fraîche

½ cup/120 ml reduced-sodium chicken broth

1 bunch fresh tarragon, for garnish (optional)

1. Divide the butter evenly between two bowls. Cover and refrigerate one bowl; set the other aside at room temperature for basting the pork.

2. Arrange a rack at center position and preheat the oven to 350°F/180°C/gas 4.

3. Using a sharp paring knife, make slits over the entire surface of the pork and insert the garlic slivers. Stand the roast on a rack in a large roasting pan/tray. Brush one-third of the room-temperature butter over the meat. Cover the bone tips with foil.

4. If you have a soufflé dish that is just slightly smaller than the cavity of the roast, place it in the center to help the roast hold its shape as it cooks. Do not worry if you don't have one as the pork can be roasted without it. Roast the pork until a meat thermometer inserted into the thickest part of the center of the roast registers 150 to 155°F/65 to 68°C, for 2 to 2½ hours. Watch carefully as the cooking time can vary depending on the size of the roast (see cooking tip). Brush the roast with some of the butter every 20 minutes.

5. Transfer the roast to a platter, tent it loosely with foil, and let rest for 25 minutes before carving.

6. Meanwhile, with an electric mixer on medium speed, beat the chilled butter until smooth and creamy, then whisk in the crème fraîche until just incorporated. Transfer to a serving bowl.

7. Skim off and discard any fat in the roasting pan/tray. Place the pan over 1 to 2 burners on medium-high heat; add the broth and bring to a boil, scraping up any browned bits into the liquids. Cook for only 1 to 2 minutes, then transfer the sauce (which will be quite thin) to a serving bowl.

8. If using the soufflé dish, remove with potholders from the center of the roast. Discard the foil on the bone tips. If desired, garnish the roast with several bouquets of tarragon. To serve, slice the roast into chops and top each with pan juices and with a dollop of the whipped butter.

SIDES: For an impressive appearance, fill the cavity of the roast with a double or triple recipe of Best-Ever Mashed Potatoes (page 138) or with Wild Rice with Roasted Grapes and Walnuts (page 155). Add some tender green beans tossed in butter and sprinkled with fleur de sel to complete the menu.

LEFTOVER TIP: Extra chops can be reheated and topped with leftover Tarragon-Mustard Butter. Heat the chops in a microwave just to warm and enjoy with a green salad.

MARKET NOTE: Ask the butcher to tie together two racks with 8 ribs each (each rack should be about 4 lb/1.8 kg) to form the crown roast. You should have about 8 lb/3.6 kg total, but the weight can vary depending on the size of racks available. Also make certain that the butcher removes the feather and chine bones so that you will be able to slice the rack into individual chops. The racks should be frenched, which means that all the meat between the rib bones is trimmed away for a neat appearance.

COOKING TIP: The most important element in cooking this roast is getting the pork to the correct internal temperature. Many other variables (especially the weight and size of the racks) affect the cooking time. In an effort to get the correct temperature, always place the thermometer in the center of this roast (inside the bones). That area takes the longest to cook.

Four-Hour Roasted Pork Shoulder for Pulled Pork Sandwiches

I grew up in the American South, where pulled pork barbecue sandwiches were at the top of the food pyramid. My parents thought nothing of driving well over an hour to indulge in the best pulled pork in the region. The pork featured here could easily rival those of my youth. A boneless shoulder is rubbed with a handful of seasonings, and then roasted slow and low until it is so tender it can be "pulled" apart with table forks. When ready to serve, you mound the pork atop soft hamburger buns, then slather on the simple homemade barbecue sauce and some cole slaw, if desired.

Makes 12 large sandwiches

COST: Inexpensive

PREP TIME:
1 hour, 15 minutes, including making the barbecue sauce

START-TO-FINISH TIME:
8 to 11 hours

One 4½-lb/2-kg boneless pork shoulder (also called a Boston butt), tied

2 tbsp chili powder

1 tbsp ground cumin

1 tsp light brown sugar

½ tsp onion powder

Pinch cayenne pepper

12 hamburger buns

Homemade Barbecue Sauce (page 175)

1. Pat the pork dry with paper towels/absorbent paper and place on a work surface. Combine the chili powder, cumin, brown sugar, onion powder, and cayenne. Rub the spice mixture over all surfaces of the roast. Wrap the roast in plastic wrap/cling film and refrigerate for at least 3 hours or up to 8 hours.

2. Arrange a rack at center position and preheat the oven to 300°F/150°C/gas 2.

3. Remove the plastic wrap/cling film and place the pork on a rack in a roasting pan/tray that is large enough to hold it comfortably.

4. Roast until you can pierce all surfaces of the pork very easily with a sharp knife and a thermometer registers 190°F/88°C when inserted into the thickest part of the roast, for 4 to 4¼ hours. Remove the roast from the oven and let rest for 20 minutes.

continued...

5. Using two table forks, "pull" the pork into shreds. (The pork can be prepared 2 days ahead; cool, cover, and refrigerate. Spread on a rimmed baking sheet/tray, sprinkle lightly with a little water, cover with foil, and reheat in a 350°F/180°C/gas 4 oven until warm, about 20 minutes.)

6. Serve the pork mounded on hamburger buns and drizzled generously with Homemade Barbecue Sauce. Pass extra sauce separately.

SIDES: Cole slaw and baked beans are favorite sides for these sandwiches, and Skillet Summer Corn (page 154) would also make a fine addition.

LEFTOVER TIP: Both the pork and the barbecue sauce freeze well. Pack each separately, and you'll have the makings for these sandwiches on hand whenever you crave real Southern barbecue.

Racks of Pork with Apple Chutney

Plenty of cooks have made racks of lamb, but few have indulged in succulent racks of pork. The latter make an impressive presentation and are quite reasonably priced. In the following recipe, pork racks are brushed with curry oil (a simple combo of olive oil and curry powder) and roasted on a bed of onion wedges. When done, these dark golden racks are served with their bones intertwined, surrounded by the slightly charred onions and accompanied by homemade apple chutney. When sliced, the pork yields extra-large chops.

Serves 10

COST: Moderate

PREP TIME:
1 hour, 15 minutes, including making the chutney

START-TO-FINISH TIME:
4 hours, 15 minutes, including resting time for the cooked meat

½ cup/120 ml olive oil

4 tsp curry powder

2 racks of pork with 5 ribs each, about 3 lb/1.4 kg per rack (see market note, page 59)

1½ lb/680 g medium red onions

Kosher salt

Freshly ground black pepper

Apple Chutney (page 162)

1. In a small bowl, whisk together the olive oil and curry powder. Brush all surfaces of the pork with half of the oil mixture; reserve the remaining oil. Let racks rest at cool room temperature for 1½ hours.

2. Arrange a rack at center position and preheat the oven to 350°F/180°C/gas 4.

3. Peel the onions and cut them into 1-in/2.5-cm thick wedges, leaving root ends intact. Salt and pepper the racks of pork on all sides.

4. Set a large, heavy, flameproof roasting pan/tray over 1 or 2 burners on medium-high heat. When hot, add one rack, fat-side down, and brown on all sides, for about 4 to 5 minutes. Remove and repeat with the remaining rack. Return the racks to the roasting pan/tray and arrange them facing each other with the bone ends pointing up, fat-sides out, and the bones intertwined. Scatter the onions around the pork and toss with the reserved curry oil.

continued…

5. Roast the pork until a meat thermometer inserted into the center of the racks registers 150°F/65°C and the onions are softened and browned around the edges, for about 1 hour.

6. Remove the racks from the pan, arrange them with the bones intertwined on a platter, and surround with the onions. Cover the racks and onions loosely with foil and let rest for 20 minutes.

7. When ready to serve, slice the racks into chops (which will be extra-large), sprinkle each with some salt, and top with some Apple Chutney. Garnish with a few onions.

SIDES: Serve the racks with Best-Ever Mashed Potatoes (page 138) and Honey-Glazed Carrots and Parsnips (page 145) or try them with Wild Rice with Roasted Grapes and Walnuts (page 155) and blanched green beans dusted with fleur de sel.

LEFTOVER TIP: For a great sandwich, thinly slice any remaining pork and mound on baguette or sourdough slices. Spoon some chutney on top of the pork and add some shaved white cheddar.

MARKET NOTE: Ask the butcher to prepare the racks by removing the feather and chine bones so that you will be able to slice the racks into individual chops. Also ask the butcher to french the racks, which means that the meat between the rib bones is trimmed away for a neat appearance. A thin layer of fat should cover the exterior of the ribs to keep the meat beneath moist as it roasts, but other excess fat should be trimmed.

Chili-Roasted Baby Backs with Homemade Barbecue Sauce

These baby back ribs are rubbed with a trio of peppers (chili powder, chipotle chili powder, and black pepper) along with other seasonings, then roasted for a couple of hours. During their last minutes in the oven, the ribs are brushed with a rich, dark barbecue sauce. When done, the glistening ribs have great depth of flavor and are tender to the bone. Plan on eating them with your fingers with plenty of napkins nearby!

Serves 6 to 8

COST: Inexpensive

PREP TIME: 10 minutes, plus 1 hour to make the Homemade Barbecue Sauce

START-TO-FINISH TIME: 4 hours, 45 minutes, including resting time for the cooked meat

4 baby back rib racks, about 2 to 2½ lb/910 g to 1.2 kg each (see market note, page 62)

½ cup/120 ml cider vinegar

4 tbsp/55 g chili powder

2 tbsp ground cumin

1 tbsp light brown sugar

1½ tsp garlic salt

1 tsp chipotle chili powder

½ tsp freshly ground black pepper

Homemade Barbecue Sauce (page 175)

1. With a sharp knife, score (making long slashes about 1 in/2.5 cm apart) the white membrane on the underside of the ribs. Place the ribs on a large, rimmed nonreactive baking sheet/tray and brush all over with the vinegar. Refrigerate, uncovered, for 2 hours.

2. Arrange a rack at center position and preheat the oven to 350°F/180°C/gas 4. Have ready two large, rimmed baking sheets/trays lined with foil.

3. In a bowl, mix together the chili powder, cumin, brown sugar, garlic salt, chipotle chili powder, and black pepper. Rub the mixture over both sides of the ribs.

4. Arrange the ribs in a single layer meat-side up, on the baking sheets/trays. Roast for 1¾ hours. Watch carefully and cover the ribs loosely with foil if the meat begins to brown too quickly.

continued...

5. Remove from the oven and brush both sides of the ribs with 1 cup/240 ml of the barbecue sauce. Roast for 10 minutes, and then brush both sides of ribs with another 1 cup/240 ml of the sauce. Roast for 15 minutes longer.

6. Remove the ribs from oven, cover them loosely with foil, and let rest for 15 minutes. Cut the ribs between the bones into 3 to 4 rib sections and mound on a platter. Serve with the remaining sauce.

SIDES: Year-round you can serve these ribs with your favorite baked beans and coleslaw, but in the summer you might like to offer them with potato salad and corn on the cob.

LEFTOVER TIP: Any leftover ribs can be cut into individual ribs and quickly reheated in the microwave for a few seconds, then used as very hearty appetizers.

MARKET NOTE: The head butcher at the store where I purchase my pork is an enthusiastic fan of baby backs. He says there is often less meat on this cut than on traditional spareribs, but the taste is better. Baby backs come from the top part of the rib cage and are shorter and curved, while spareribs are cut from farther down, near the belly, and are longer.

Ham with an Orange Marmalade Glaze and Rhubarb Chutney

This is an updated version of classic baked ham. Powdered ginger adds extra zest to a glaze made with marmalade and sharp mustard, while spiced rhubarb chutney with sweet and tart accents pairs superbly with the cooked pork. You can serve this delectable ham warm or at room temperature.

Serves 8

COST: Moderate

PREP TIME: 40 minutes, including making the chutney

START-TO-FINISH TIME: 3 hours, including resting time for cooked meat

SIDES: Golden Potato Gratin (page 141) and Green Beans with Caramelized Shallots (page 151) would make savory sides.

LEFTOVER TIPS: Use sliced ham/gammon for sandwiches made with whole-wheat or a crusty baguette. Top the ham/gammon with some rhubarb chutney and watercress. You could also dice leftover ham/gammon and combine it with sliced cooked asparagus and grated Gruyère cheese as the filling for an omelet or a savory tart.

¾ cup/240 g orange marmalade

6 tbsp/90 ml Dijon mustard

1½ tsp ground ginger

1 fully cooked semi-boneless ham/gammon, 7 to 8 lb/3.2 to 3.6 kg (from the shank or butt end)

1 bunch fresh watercress

Rhubarb Chutney (page 163)

1. Arrange a rack at lower position and preheat the oven to 325°F/165°C/gas 3.

2. Whisk the marmalade, mustard, and ginger in a heavy medium saucepan set over medium heat until the marmalade has liquefied, for 1 minute. Remove from the heat and set aside.

3. Trim any tough rind and fat from the upper side of the ham/gammon, leaving a ¼-in/6-mm layer of fat. Using a long sharp knife, score the fat in a 1-in-/2.5-cm-wide diamond pattern. Place the ham/gammon in a roasting pan/tray and roast for 1 hour, and then brush the top and sides of the ham/gammon generously with some of the marmalade-mustard glaze.

4. Continue to roast the ham/gammon, brushing it with some of the glaze every 15 minutes, until a thermometer inserted into the thickest part registers 140°F/60°C, for 45 minutes to 1 hour more.

5. When done, remove the ham/gammon to a carving board, tent loosely with foil, and let rest for 15 minutes.

6. To serve, slice the ham/gammon and arrange overlapping slices on a platter. Brush the slices with any remaining glaze. Garnish the platter with several bouquets of watercress and serve the ham/gammon, either warm or at room temperature, with a bowl of Rhubarb Chutney.

Ham Roasted with White Wine, Shallots, and Carrots

This recipe is based on a French technique in which a fully cooked ham is braised in the oven in an aromatic mix of white wine, broth, and root vegetables. For this version, the ham is brushed with an apricot and mustard glaze during the last few minutes of roasting to give it a glistening appearance. The fork-tender slices are napped with a rich sauce prepared from the pan drippings. This is definitely a special-occasion main course that could easily become the star attraction of an Easter or Christmas menu.

Serves 6 to 8

COST: Moderate

PREP TIME: 20 minutes

START-TO-FINISH TIME:
2 hours, 35 minutes

4½ tbsp/62 g unsalted butter, at room temperature

1 tbsp vegetable oil

¾ lb/340 g baby carrots, halved crosswise (see market note)

¾ lb/340 g (about 12 medium) shallots, peeled and halved lengthwise

Kosher salt

Freshly ground black pepper

2 cups/480 ml dry white wine

3 cups/720 ml reduced-sodium chicken broth

1 fully cooked boneless or semi-boneless cooked ham/gammon, 5 to 6 lb/1.8 to 2.3 kg (see cooking tip)

6 flat-leaf parsley sprigs, plus extra for the garnish

6 long thyme sprigs, plus extra for the garnish

3 bay leaves, broken in half

¼ cup/80 g apricot jam

4 tsp Dijon mustard

3 tbsp flour

¾ cup/180 ml heavy/double cream

1 tbsp minced fresh thyme

1. Arrange a rack at lower position and preheat the oven to 350°F/180°C/gas 4.

2. Heat 1½ tbsp of the butter and the oil in a large, heavy roasting pan/tray set over 1 to 2 burners on medium-high heat until hot. Add the carrots and shallots and sauté, stirring, until lightly browned, for 5 to 6 minutes. Salt and pepper the vegetables. Pour 1 cup/240 ml of the wine and 1 cup/240 ml of the broth into the pan and bring the mixture to a simmer over high heat. Remove the pan from the heat and place the ham/gammon, fat-side up, on top of the vegetables. Add the parsley sprigs, thyme sprigs, and bay leaves. Tent the pan/tray with a large sheet of foil, tucking in the edges and being careful not to let the foil touch the ham.

3. Roast the ham/gammon, basting every 20 minutes with pan juices, until tender when pierced with a knife and a thermometer registers 140°F/60°C when inserted into the center, for about 1½ hours. When you baste the ham/gammon, use mitts to carefully remove the foil so that you do not burn yourself. Remove the pan from the oven and raise the oven temperature to 450°F/230°C/gas 8.

4. In a small bowl, whisk together the apricot jam and 2 tsp of the mustard until blended. Brush over the ham/gammon, return it to the oven, and roast, uncovered, for 15 minutes.

5. Remove the ham/gammon to a cutting board, tent loosely with foil, and let rest for 15 minutes while you make the sauce. Remove all the solids (herbs and vegetables) from the pan with a slotted spoon and discard. Skim off and discard any fat in the pan.

6. Mix the remaining 3 tbsp butter with the flour in a small bowl until blended into a paste. Place the roasting pan/tray over 1 or 2 burners over high heat and add the remaining 1 cup/240 ml wine, remaining 2 cups/480 ml broth, cream, minced thyme, and remaining 2 tsp mustard. Bring to a simmer, then whisk in the butter/flour mixture a little at a time, until the sauce thickens and reduces to 3 cups/ 720 ml, for about 10 minutes. Season the sauce with salt and pepper.

7. To serve, slice the ham/gammon and arrange overlapping slices on a serving platter. Spoon some of the sauce over the ham/gammon, garnish the platter with bouquets of parsley and thyme sprigs, and pass the remaining sauce separately.

SIDES: For a spring menu, offer Best-Ever Mashed Potatoes Creamy Goat Cheese and Thyme variation (page 138) and 5-Minute Roasted Sugar Snap Peas (page 149). For fall or winter dinners, try roasted baby red potatoes or buttered noodles plus tender green beans sprinkled with sea salt.

LEFTOVER TIPS: Remaining slices of this ham/ gammon can be julienned or diced and tossed with buttered noodles; ladle some leftover sauce over the pasta and sprinkle with grated Parmesan. Or make sandwiches on crusty country bread with ham/gammon, farmhouse cheddar, and peppery watercress.

MARKET NOTE: Peeled baby carrots (about 2 in/5 cm long and less than 1 in/2.5 cm in diameter), available in the produce section of supermarkets, are a great time-saver. If unavailable, peel small, slim carrots and cut into 1-in/2.5-cm lengths.

COOKING TIP: You'll get slightly more ham with a boneless cut.

LAMB AND VEAL

Keys for Cooking to Perfection

Whenever I include roast lamb or veal in one of my cooking classes, I am often surprised to learn that many students are unfamiliar with these meats. Some tell me that lamb appeared only occasionally on their family table, and that it was often tough and dry, a sure sign of overcooking. The store-bought, bright green mint jelly that accompanied these roasts did not add much to their appeal. Veal is viewed differently; most students have enjoyed tender veal dishes at their favorite restaurants but shy away from cooking this meat at home. With steep price tags attached to many cuts of veal, it can seem intimidating. As a teacher, my goal is to banish these misconceptions (and the green jelly) and to share my love of lamb and veal with home cooks.

Let's start with lamb. The golden rule is to not over-cook it. Roast lamb is best when a thermometer registers 130 to 135°F/55 to 57°C and the meat inside is rosy pink.

As for variety, there are plenty of choices. A leg of lamb, either with the bone in or removed, makes a glorious main course, as you'll discover in Orange-Studded Leg of Lamb with Spring-Herbs Butter, or Boneless Leg of Lamb with Tomato-Olive Relish. Nothing could be more impressive (or easier to prepare!) for a special occasion than Racks of Lamb with New Potatoes and Mint Pesto.

When it comes to veal, knowing which cuts to buy and how to prepare them is the secret. Veal shanks are a good value and burst with flavor, especially when they are cooked ossobuco-style until fork-tender as in Veal Shanks Roasted in Red Wine with Tomatoes and Sage. Top round is the section from which veal scallops or scaloppine are thinly sliced, but my butcher confided to me that a roast cut from this area is very tender and has no waste. Summertime Olive-Studded Roast Veal resulted from this revelation. Veal chops can be roasted instead of sautéed with outstanding results. The Veal Chops with a New Orleans Stuffing are pan-seared, then conveniently finished in the oven.

In the pages that follow, you will find diverse and tempting recipes for lamb and veal roasts. Set aside your preconceptions about these meats, delve in, and savor every mouthful.

Orange-Studded Leg of Lamb with Spring-Herbs Butter

A simple herbed butter, scented with fresh tarragon and mint, is the big flavoring agent for this leg of lamb studded with slivers of orange peel. The butter is brushed over the lamb before roasting, then used to baste it while it is in the oven. Finally, this aromatic butter is combined with the pan drippings to make a flavorful sauce.

Serves 8

COST: Moderate

PREP TIME: 25 minutes, including making the butter

START-TO-FINISH TIME: 2 hours, 20 minutes, including resting time for cooked meat

One 6½-lb/3-kg leg of lamb with bone, trimmed of excess fat

1 tbsp very thin, 1-in/2.5-cm-long strips of orange peel (see cooking tip, page 70), plus 2 tsp grated orange zest

Kosher salt

Freshly ground black pepper

2 tbsp olive oil

Spring-Herbs Butter (page 172)

2 cups/480 ml dry red wine

1½ cups/360 ml reduced-sodium chicken broth

Fresh tarragon and mint sprigs, for garnish

1. With a small, sharp knife, make 1-in-/2.5-cm-deep slits all over the lamb and insert 1 or 2 orange peel slivers into each. (The lamb can be studded 1 day ahead; cover with plastic wrap/cling film and refrigerate.)

2. Arrange a rack at lower position and preheat the oven to 450°F/230°C/gas 8.

3. Sprinkle the lamb with salt and pepper. Heat the oil in a large flameproof roasting pan/tray set over 2 burners on medium-high heat. When the oil is hot, brown the lamb on all sides, for 7 to 8 minutes. Remove the pan from the heat and brush all over with 2 tbsp of the Spring-Herbs Butter.

4. Roast the lamb for 15 minutes, then brush with another 2 tbsp of the butter. Reduce the heat to 350°F/180°C/gas 4 and continue to roast the lamb until an instant-read thermometer inserted into thickest part of the meat registers 135 to 140°F/57 to 60°C for medium-rare, for about 55 minutes more. (Cooking time can vary depending on the thickness of the roast, so start to check the temperature after 30 minutes.) Transfer the lamb to a carving board, tent loosely with foil, and let rest for 30 minutes.

continued...

5. Spoon off and discard any fat from the juices in the roasting pan/tray. Place the pan over high heat. Add the wine and broth and bring to a boil, whisking constantly to scrape up any browned bits on the bottom of the pan into the liquids. Boil until the sauce reduces to 2 cups/480 ml, for 5 minutes. Whisk in the remaining 4 tbsp/55 g herb butter and the orange zest. Season with salt and pepper.

6. To serve, slice the lamb and arrange on a platter. Nap with some sauce and pass remaining sauce separately. Garnish with tarragon and mint sprigs.

SIDES: Serve this beautiful leg of lamb with Spring Vegetables Tossed in Spring-Herbs Butter (page 150). The same butter is called for in both dishes. For a striking presentation, surround the roast with the vegetables.

LEFTOVER TIP: Fill pita pockets with leftover slices of lamb along with some peppery watercress and thinly sliced cucumbers. Add a dollop of yogurt or mayo for a tasty sandwich.

COOKING TIP: To make the orange peel slivers, use a vegetable peeler to peel strips from an orange, taking care to remove just the peel and not any of the bitter white pith beneath. If any white remains on the orange peel, scrape it off with a sharp knife. Cut the orange peel into thin julienne strips about 1 in/2.5 cm long.

Boneless Leg of Lamb with Tomato-Olive Relish

If you want to serve a roast that's stress-free, this boneless leg of lamb is the answer. It is placed in a self-sealing plastic bag, covered with a simple marinade for several hours, then roasted in about 30 minutes. Instead of a last-minute sauce, the succulent slices of lamb are served with a vibrant Mediterranean relish that can be assembled well ahead.

Serves 5 to 6

COST: Moderate

PREP TIME: 35 minutes, including making the Tomato-Olive Relish

START-TO-FINISH TIME: 4 hours, 40 minutes to 9 hours, 40 minutes, including resting time for the cooked meat

1 boneless leg of lamb with a thin layer of fat, 2½ to 3 lb/1.2 to 1.4 kg, tied
½ cup/120 ml dry red wine
¼ cup/60 ml olive oil, plus more as needed
2 medium garlic cloves, smashed
1 tsp fennel seeds, crushed (see cooking tip)
½ tsp kosher salt
½ tsp freshly ground black pepper
Tomato-Olive Relish (page 167)

SIDES: Best-Ever Mashed Potatoes Provencal Basil or the Creamy Goat Cheese and Thyme variations (page 138) and sliced sautéed zucchini/courgette would make delicious garnishes for the lamb. You could also serve it with Sautéed Spinach (page 148), using goat cheese instead of the blue cheese, and some buttered couscous.

LEFTOVER TIP: For sandwiches, slice leftover lamb thinly and place in pita pockets along with some of the relish and crumbled feta.

COOKING TIP: To crush fennel seeds, place them in a self-sealing plastic bag and pound with a meat pounder or rolling pin. You can also crush them using a mortar and pestle or grind them in a small spice grinder.

1. Place the lamb in a large, self-sealing plastic bag. In a medium bowl, stir together the wine, oil, garlic, fennel seeds, salt, and pepper. Pour the marinade over the lamb and seal. Refrigerate the lamb for 3 to 8 hours, turning occasionally.

2. Arrange a rack at center position and preheat the oven to 400°F/200°C/gas 6.

3. Remove the lamb from the marinade and pat dry with paper towels/absorbent paper. Heat enough olive oil to lightly coat the bottom of a large, heavy, ovenproof roasting pan/tray set over medium-high heat. When the oil is hot, add the lamb and brown on all sides, for 6 to 8 minutes. Place the lamb in the oven and roast it until a thermometer registers 130°F/55°C when inserted into the thickest part of the meat, for 35 to 45 minutes, depending on the size of the roast.

4. Remove the lamb to a carving board and tent loosely with foil. Let rest for 15 minutes. Slice the meat into slices ½ in/12 mm thick, arrange them overlapping on a platter, and serve with Tomato-Olive Relish.

Corfu Lamb and Vegetables Roasted in Parchment

A few years ago I was lucky enough to go on a boat trip around the Dalmatian coast. One of the ports of call was the Greek island of Corfu, and during a short visit there, I stopped for lunch in a little taverna. The menu was Greek to me, but my waiter, both bilingual and enthusiastic, helped out, suggesting a specialty of lamb and vegetables baked in a parchment/baking paper pouch. When the dish arrived, a packet tied in twine was set on a plate in front of me. When opened, it revealed piping-hot cubes of lamb and all manner of colorful roasted vegetables. One bite and I was in heaven! The meat was fork-tender, as were carrots, potatoes, and tomatoes. Juices from the lamb and the vegetables had been released during the long, slow cooking, and had combined to form a thin but wonderfully flavorful sauce. At home, I realized how practical this dish would be for entertaining. After the packages are filled and tied, they go into the oven for 2 hours of totally unattended roasting.

Serves 4

COST: Moderate

PREP TIME: 45 minutes

START-TO-FINISH TIME:
2 hours, 50 minutes, including resting time for cooked meat

MATERIALS:
Parchment/baking paper
Kitchen twine

1½ lb/680 g boneless leg of lamb, trimmed of excess fat and cut into 1-in/2.5-cm cubes

2 medium carrots, peeled and cut on the diagonal into slices ½ in/12 mm thick

½ medium onion, peeled and cut into 8 wedges

4 small red skin potatoes (1½ oz/40 g each), scrubbed but unpeeled, cut into ½-in/12-mm wedges

1 medium tomato, halved lengthwise and cut into ½-in/12-mm wedges

1 medium red bell pepper, halved, seeded, and deribbed, with halves cut into 1-in/2.5-cm pieces

8 large garlic cloves, peeled

¼ cup/7 g baby spinach leaves

1 tsp dried oregano

1 tsp dried crushed rosemary (see cooking tip, page 19)

1 tsp kosher salt

Freshly ground black pepper

8 tbsp/120 ml olive oil

Fresh rosemary sprigs, for garnish (optional)

1. Cut out four 15-in/38-cm parchment/baking paper squares and place them on a work surface. Place one-fourth of the lamb cubes in the center of each square. Scatter one-fourth of the carrots, onion, potatoes, tomato, red pepper, and garlic cloves over the meat, then tuck one-fourth of the spinach leaves into each mixture. Sprinkle each portion with ¼ tsp oregano, ¼ tsp rosemary, ¼ tsp salt, and several grinds of black pepper, then drizzle each with 2 tbsp olive oil.

2. Pull the corners of each paper square together to make a pouch, and then tie tightly with string. Place the pouches on a rimmed baking sheet/tray. (The pouches can be filled and tied 2 hours ahead. Refrigerate and bring to room temperature 30 minutes before baking.)

3. Arrange a rack at center position and preheat the oven to 300°F/150°C/gas 2.

4. Place the baking sheet/tray with the pouches in the oven and roast for 2 hours. Remove the baking sheet/tray from the oven and let the pouches cool for 5 minutes. Transfer each pouch to a dinner plate or shallow soup bowl. For serving, untie the strings and spread open the papers. Garnish each serving with 1 or 2 rosemary sprigs, if desired.

SIDES: A classic Greek salad of crisp greens, olives, onions, tomatoes, and crumbled feta, plus some good crusty bread for sopping up the sauce, are all you need as accompaniments to this Corfu specialty.

LEFTOVER TIP: Reheat lamb and vegetables and serve atop warm couscous.

Lamb Shanks with Dates and Olives

When I included this Moroccan-style braised lamb in a cooking class, students were crazy about the melange of interesting flavors. Dates and brown sugar add sweetness, green olives and capers lend a salty note, and wine and vinegar provide a bit of tartness. After close to two hours in the oven, the lamb is so tender it practically falls off the bone.

Serves 4

COST: Moderate

PREP TIME: 15 minutes

START-TO-FINISH TIME: 2 hours, 15 minutes

2 tbsp olive oil

3½ to 4 lb/1.6 to 1.8 kg lamb shanks (see market note)

1 tbsp ground cumin

1 tbsp kosher salt

1 tbsp coarsely ground black pepper

2 tsp dried thyme

3 bay leaves, broken in half

2 sprigs plus 3 tbsp minced flat-leaf parsley

⅔ cup/98 g green Mediterranean olives, pitted or unpitted

⅓ cup/85 g capers with a little of their juice

1 cup/240 ml dry red wine

⅓ cup/75 ml red wine vinegar

⅓ cup/65 g light brown sugar

16 large Medjool dates, unpitted

¼ tsp harissa or 2 pinches of hot pepper flakes (see market note)

1. Arrange a rack at center position and preheat the oven to 375°F/190°C/gas 5.

2. Heat the oil in a large nonreactive, deep-sided pot (with a lid) set over medium-high heat. When hot, add the lamb shanks and brown on all sides, for 4 to 5 minutes. Remove the pot from the heat.

3. In a small bowl, mix together the cumin, salt, pepper, and thyme, then sprinkle this mixture over the browned lamb. Add the bay leaves, parsley sprigs, olives, and capers to the pot. Pour the wine and vinegar over the lamb, and then sprinkle the brown sugar over the mixture. Cover the pot tightly with a double thickness of foil, then with the lid.

4. Roast for 45 minutes, then remove the pot from the oven and turn the meat. Add the dates, cover again with the foil and lid, and continue to cook until the meat is fork-tender, for about 50 to 60 minutes more.

5. Remove the pot from the oven and uncover it. Stir in the harissa and 1½ cups/120 ml water. (The lamb can be prepared 2 days ahead. Cool, then cover the pot with the foil and lid, and refrigerate. Reheat, covered with foil and lid, in a 375°F/190°C/gas 5 oven until hot, for about 25 minutes.)

6. To serve, arrange the lamb shanks in a bowl or on a platter. Ladle the sauce with dates and olives over the lamb, and then sprinkle with minced parsley. With a sharp knife, slice the lamb shanks before serving. Be sure to let everyone know that there are pits in the dates and in the olives if you used unpitted ones.

SIDES: Serve this lamb with a bowl of couscous prepared with a generous pinch of saffron or turmeric, and a green salad with fresh orange segments tossed in lemon juice and olive oil.

LEFTOVER TIP: You can quickly reheat any remaining lamb shanks in the microwave. They taste even better a day or two after the initial cooking.

MARKET NOTES: Lamb shanks can vary in size, weighing anywhere from 12 to 14 oz/340 to 400 g to more than 1 lb/455 g each. Either size will work in this recipe as long as you have 3½ to 4 lb/1.6 to 1.8 kg total. The cooking time should be about the same for both.

Harissa, a paste of hot pureed peppers and spices used in Moroccan and North African cooking, is sold in specialty food stores.

Racks of Lamb with New Potatoes and Mint Pesto

This dish boasts some of spring's early harbingers—lamb, mint, and new potatoes. Beautiful racks (with their bones frenched so that they look particularly elegant) and small red potatoes are brushed with oil, mustard, and garlic, then roasted together. In place of traditional mint jelly, a fresh mint pesto accompanies the lamb.

Serves 8,
with 2 chops each

COST: Splurge

PREP TIME: 30 minutes

START-TO-FINISH TIME: 1 hour, 15 minutes, including resting time for cooked meat while the potatoes finish roasting

Mint Pesto

2 cups/55 g packed fresh mint leaves

¾ cup/180 ml olive oil

¼ cup/60 ml fresh lemon juice

4 medium garlic cloves, peeled

1 tsp kosher salt

Scant ½ tsp red pepper flakes

Lamb and Potatoes

½ cup/120 ml olive oil, plus more as needed

6 medium garlic cloves, minced

2 tbsp Dijon mustard

1¾ lb/800 g small red new potatoes (1½ in/4 cm diameter), scrubbed and quartered (unpeeled)

Kosher salt

Freshly ground black pepper

2 racks of lamb, 1½ lb/680 g each with 8 chops, trimmed and frenched (see market note, page 80)

Fresh mint sprigs, for garnish

FOR THE MINT PESTO:

Place the mint leaves, olive oil, lemon juice, garlic, salt, and red pepper flakes in a food processor or a blender. Process, pulsing machine on and off, for 45 seconds or longer until mint and garlic are finely minced and the mixture has a pesto-like consistency. Remove and set aside at cool room temperature. The pesto is best prepared no more than 1½ hours ahead for its color to remain bright green (see cooking tip). You should get about 1¼ cups/300 g.

FOR THE LAMB AND POTATOES:

1. Arrange a rack at center position and preheat the oven to 425°F/220°C/gas 7. Have ready a large, heavy, rimmed baking sheet/tray.

2. Whisk together ½ cup/120 ml olive oil, garlic, and mustard in a small bowl. Transfer ⅓ cup/75 ml of this mixture to a large bowl and add the potatoes. Toss to coat well.

3. Heat enough oil to lightly coat the bottom of a large frying pan set over medium-high heat. When quite hot, add 1 lamb rack, rounded-side down, and brown on that side only, for about 3 minutes. Remove and repeat with the other rack, adding more oil if needed. Let racks rest until cool enough to handle, for 10 minutes.

4. Transfer the racks to the baking sheet/tray and arrange them facing each other with bone ends pointing up, browned-sides out, and bones intertwined. Scatter the potatoes around the lamb. Season both the lamb and potatoes generously with salt and pepper. Brush the lamb with the remaining mustard mixture on all sides.

5. Roast the lamb and potatoes until a thermometer inserted into the center of the meat registers 130°F/55°C for medium-rare, for about 20 minutes. When the lamb is done, transfer to a platter with bones intertwined. Tent with foil and let rest for 15 minutes.

6. Continue to roast the potatoes until cooked through and crisp, stirring once, for about 15 minutes longer.

7. Surround the lamb with potatoes and garnish the platter with several bouquets of mint. Slice into chops, and serve with a bowl of the mint pesto.

SIDES: This meat-and-potatoes dish could be served with blanched asparagus or snow peas/mangetout sprinkled with snipped chives. Or try it with a watercress and cucumber salad tossed in lemon juice and olive oil.

LEFTOVER TIP: Extra chops make a nice cold lunch. Serve them at room temperature topped with some mint pesto and accompanied by toasted pita wedges. If you have any potatoes left, toss them in some vinaigrette and enjoy as a salad.

COOKING TIP: Leftover pesto can be kept refrigerated for 3 to 4 days and will still taste delicious even though it will lose its bright green color.

Racks of Lamb with Whipped Goat Cheese and Roasted Cherry Tomatoes

This is an elegant yet simple way to prepare racks of lamb. Marinated in a classic combo of lemon, garlic, and olive oil, these racks are browned quickly and roasted until rosy pink inside. What makes this dish unusual are the interesting garnishes. Roasted cherry tomatoes and dollops of creamy whipped goat cheese seasoned with lemon and dill are perfect partners for the lamb.

Serves 8 with
2 chops each

COST: Splurge

PREP TIME: 1 hour, including making the Whipped Goat Cheese and marinating the lamb

START-TO-FINISH TIME: 1 hour, 50 minutes, including resting time for the cooked meat.

Whipped Goat Cheese

1 cup/225 g creamy fresh goat cheese

¼ cup/60 ml olive oil

4 tsp minced dill, plus 2 or 3 sprigs for garnish

2 tsp grated lemon zest

Lamb

¼ cup/60 ml olive oil, plus more for sautéing the racks

2 tbsp fresh lemon juice

4 medium garlic cloves, smashed and peeled

Kosher salt

Freshly ground black pepper

2 racks of lamb, about 1½ lb/680 g each, trimmed and frenched (see market note, page 80)

1½ cups/270 g cherry or grape tomatoes

FOR THE WHIPPED GOAT CHEESE:
Put the cheese in a medium bowl and, with an electric mixer on medium speed, beat for 30 seconds, then gradually, a little at a time, beat in the olive oil. Stir in the dill and lemon zest. The mixture should be light and fluffy. (This can be prepared 3 hours ahead; cover and refrigerate. Bring to room temperature 30 minutes before serving.)

FOR THE LAMB:

1. Whisk together the olive oil, lemon juice, garlic, 1 tsp salt, and 1½ tsp pepper in a shallow nonreactive pan. Add the lamb racks, turning to coat well. Marinate the lamb at room temperature, turning the racks occasionally, for 45 minutes. (If you want to marinate the lamb longer, cover and refrigerate for up to 3 hours. Bring to room temperature 30 minutes before cooking.)

2. Arrange a rack at center position and preheat the oven to 425°F/220°C/gas 7.

3. Remove the lamb from the marinade and salt and pepper each rack on both sides. Add enough olive oil to lightly coat the bottom of a large, heavy, flameproof roasting pan/ tray, and place it over 1 or 2 burners set on medium-high

continued...

heat. When hot, add 1 lamb rack, rounded-side down, to the pan and brown on that side only, for about 3 minutes. Remove and repeat with the remaining rack, adding more oil if needed. Pour out any drippings in the pan. Let racks rest until cool enough to handle, for 10 minutes. Arrange the racks in the roasting pan/tray facing each other with bone ends pointing up, browned-sides out, and bones intertwined. Roast until a thermometer inserted into the center of the lamb reads 130°F/55°C for medium-rare, for about 20 minutes.

4. Remove the racks to a platter with bones intertwined, tent loosely with foil, and let rest for 15 minutes. Retain the oven temperature and add the tomatoes to the roasting pan/tray. Return the pan to the oven and roast the tomatoes until just hot and starting to shrink, for about 5 minutes.

5. Garnish the racks with tomatoes, and serve them with a bowl of the Whipped Goat Cheese. Slice into chops and spoon the cheese atop each chop.

SIDES: Golden Potato Gratin (page 141) and sautéed zucchini/courgette or blanched tender green beans could round out the menu.

LEFTOVER TIP: If you have any Whipped Goat Cheese left, it makes a great spread for a sandwich or a good topping for toasted pita wedges served as appetizers.

MARKET NOTE: Ask the butcher to french the racks, which means that the meat between the rib bones is removed. Also, a thin layer of fat should cover the ribs to keep them moist as they roast, but other excess fat should be trimmed.

Roast Veal with Tarragon-Mustard Butter

You won't find this roast waiting in the packaged meats section of your supermarket; a boneless top loin is a specialty cut that you will need to order from your butcher. Although it comes with a noticeable price tag, there is absolutely no waste in this tender, delicious cut. The best way to cook this veal roast is simply, as in the following recipe, where it is studded with garlic, then browned and placed in the oven for about 40 minutes. The exceptionally flavorful Tarragon-Mustard Butter is used to baste the veal while it roasts and as a garnish for the beautiful, warm slices.

Serves 5 to 6

COST: Splurge

PREP TIME: 25 minutes, including making the Tarragon-Mustard Butter

START-TO-FINISH TIME: 1 hour, 30 minutes, including resting time for cooked meat

SIDES: Sautéed Spinach with Blue Cheese and Hazelnuts (page 148) and buttered new potatoes would make delectable accompaniments for this roast, or serve it with the Golden Potato Gratin (page 141) and roasted or blanched asparagus.

LEFTOVER TIP: This sliced veal is superb in a sandwich. Top good whole-wheat bread with veal, sliced tomatoes, and creamy goat cheese.

MARKET NOTE: Ask your butcher for a boneless top loin veal roast with a thin layer of fat on top and have it tied. The roast will be long and slender in shape, about 10 in/25 cm long by 3 in/7.5 cm in diameter, depending on how the butcher cuts it.

Tarragon-Mustard Butter (page 172)
1 boneless top loin veal roast,
   2 to 2½ lb/910 g to 1.2 kg (see market note)
2 medium garlic cloves,
   peeled and cut into thin slivers
Kosher salt
Freshly ground black pepper
2 tbsp olive oil, plus more as needed

1. Put half of the Tarragon-Mustard Butter in a small, shallow bowl to serve with the cooked roast; cover and leave at room temperature.

2. Arrange a rack at center position and preheat the oven to 350°F/180°C/gas 4.

3. Pat the veal dry with paper towels/absorbent paper. Using a sharp paring knife, make slits all over the entire surface of the roast, and insert the garlic slivers. Season the roast generously with salt and pepper.

4. Heat the oil in a medium, heavy roasting pan/tray set over 1 to 2 burners at medium-high heat until hot. Add the veal and brown on all sides, for 4 to 5 minutes; add more oil if necessary. Spoon off and discard any excess fat in the roasting pan/tray. Brush the roast on the top and sides with a generous tablespoon of Tarragon-Mustard Butter.

5. Roast the veal until a thermometer inserted into the center of the meat registers 135 to 140°F/57 to 60°C, for 30 to 40 minutes. Baste the roast with a tablespoon of the butter every 10 minutes. When done, brush meat with any remaining basting butter, and then transfer the roast to a cutting board, tent loosely with foil, and let rest for 15 minutes.

6. Cut the roast into slices ½ in/12 mm thick and arrange them overlapping on a serving platter. Serve the warm veal slices topped with dollops of the reserved butter.

Summertime Olive-Studded Roast Veal

This boneless top round roast (cut from the same part of the veal used for scaloppine) is a special order, but definitely worth the effort. The meat is studded with slivered dark olives and garlic, and then roasted and chilled. The cold veal slices, topped with a piquant Tomato-Olive Relish, make a stunning centerpiece for warm-weather meals. Besides its great look and taste, this roast has another important advantage. There's absolutely no last-minute work, since both the veal and the relish are prepared well in advance.

Serves 6

COST: Splurge

PREP TIME: 15 minutes

START-TO-FINISH TIME: 3 to 4 hours, including resting and chilling time for the cooked meat

---

One 2-lb/920-g boneless top round veal roast, tied

¼ cup/40 g pitted and slivered kalamata olives

2 large garlic cloves, cut into thin slivers

Olive oil for coating the roasting pan/tray

Kosher salt

Freshly ground black pepper

1 cup/240 ml reduced-sodium chicken broth, plus more as needed

1 cup/240 ml dry white wine, plus more as needed

Juice of ½ lemon

Tomato-Olive Relish (page 167)

Fresh basil sprigs for garnish

SIDES: Make a salad of tender green beans and thinly sliced fennel tossed in lemon juice and olive oil and seasoned with plenty of black pepper. A baguette or a good peasant country loaf could complete the meal.

LEFTOVER TIP: Extra sliced veal and relish can be paired for a great sandwich. Pack them in a pita pocket or mound open-faced on a baguette slice and sprinkle with crumbled feta.

---

1. Arrange a rack at center position and preheat the oven to 350°F/180°C/gas 4.

2. Using a sharp paring knife, make slits all over the entire surface of the roast and insert the olive and garlic slivers.

3. Generously coat a large, flameproof roasting pan/tray with oil. Place over 1 to 2 burners and heat over medium-high heat. Add the roast and brown well on all sides, for 5 to 6 minutes. Remove the roast, salt and pepper it well, and place it on a rack in the same roasting pan/tray.

4. Place the veal in the oven and roast it for 15 minutes. Then, combine the broth and wine and baste the roast with ½ cup/120 ml of this mixture. Roast the veal for 15 minutes more and baste with another ½ cup/120 ml of the broth-wine mixture and pour the lemon juice over the meat.

5. Continue to roast the veal until a thermometer inserted into the center of the roast registers 130 to 135°F/55 to 57°C for medium, for about 45 minutes more, basting every 15 minutes with ½ cup/120 ml of the broth-wine mixture. (If necessary use equal amounts of extra broth and wine.) Remove the roast to a platter. Cool it to room temperature, and then cover and refrigerate until cold, for 1 to 2 hours. (The roast can be prepared 1 day ahead.)

6. To serve, slice the cold roast into thin slices (⅛- to ¼-in/ 3- to 6-mm thick). Arrange the veal in overlapping slices on a platter and spoon some Tomato-Olive Relish down the center. Garnish with basil sprigs. Pass the remaining relish in a bowl.

Veal Chops with a New Orleans Stuffing

My grandparents lived just north of New Orleans, so I visited the Big Easy often as a youngster. Later I spent my college years there. If you stay for any time at all in this unique American city, you'll fall in love with the vibrant flavors of its cuisine. In these luscious roasted veal chops, spicy andouille sausage and a splash of Tabasco sauce lend a New Orleans taste to the stuffing.

Serves 4

COST: Splurge

PREP TIME: 20 minutes, including making the fresh bread crumbs

START-TO-FINISH TIME: About 50 minutes, including resting time for cooked meat

MATERIALS: Short wooden skewers, soaked in water for 30 minutes (see cooking tip)

1½ tbsp olive oil, plus more as needed

1½ tbsp unsalted butter

2 oz/55 g andouille sausage, cut into ¼-in/6-mm dice

¼ cup/30 g chopped green/spring onions, including 2 in/5 cm of green stems

1½ tsp finely minced garlic

2 packed cups (2 oz/55 g) baby spinach, coarsely chopped

¼ tsp hot sauce

1 cup/55 g fresh sourdough bread crumbs (see cooking tip, page 49)

Kosher salt

Freshly ground black pepper

4 veal rib chops, 10 to 12 oz/280 to 340 g each, and 1¼ to 1½ in/3 to 4 cm thick, trimmed of excess fat

1. In a medium, heavy frying pan set over medium-high heat, heat the olive oil and butter until the butter has melted. Add the andouille sausage and sauté, stirring, for 2 minutes. Add the green/spring onions and garlic and sauté, stirring, for 1 minute. Add the spinach and hot sauce and cook, stirring, until the spinach has wilted, for about 2 minutes. Stir in the bread crumbs and cook until they are golden, for about 2 minutes. Season with salt and pepper. Transfer the mixture to a medium bowl and cool completely.

2. Lay a veal chop on a clean work surface. Using a sharp knife, cut horizontally, making a pocket from the outside edge of the meat all the way to the bone and along the entire length of the chop. Repeat with the remaining chops. Stuff each chop with 2 to 3 tbsp of the stuffing (you may have some stuffing left over) and close the chops with wooden skewers. Salt and pepper the chops on both sides. (The chops can be prepared 4 hours ahead; cover and refrigerate.)

3. Arrange a rack at center position and preheat the oven to 450°F/230°C/gas 8.

4. Heat enough oil to generously coat the bottom of a large, ovenproof frying pan and place over medium-high heat. When oil is very hot, add the chops and sear for 2 minutes. Turn and sear for 1 minute on the other side. Transfer the frying pan to the oven and roast until a thermometer inserted into the thickest part of the chops registers 135°F/ 57°C, for 6 to 8 minutes. Remove from the oven and let rest for 5 minutes. Using mitts or a dish/tea towel so that you do not burn your fingers, carefully pull out and discard the skewers.

5. Serve the chops with any juices in the pan drizzled over them.

SIDES: Green Beans with Caramelized Shallots (page 151), and a salad of mixed greens dressed in lemon and olive oil would make fine garnishes to these rich chops.

LEFTOVER TIP: If you have any extra stuffing, fill scooped-out tomato halves with it. Brush the tomatoes with olive oil and bake in a 350°F/180°C/gas 4 oven until tomatoes are tender and stuffing is warm, about 20 minutes.

COOKING TIP: Use the shortest wooden skewers you can find for securing the stuffing in the chops. If you only have long ones, use kitchen scissors to snip off several inches so that they are about 6 in/15 cm. Even though the skewers will protrude awkwardly when used to close the chops, you can still easily sear the veal.

Veal Shanks Roasted in Red Wine with Tomatoes and Sage

These veal shanks, prepared ossobuco style, are cut crosswise into round pieces, and then cooked in an aromatic mixture of vegetables, broth, and wine. In this version, the veal simmers in the oven instead of on the stovetop, and, when done, the tender shanks are served with buttered fettuccine in place of traditional risotto. This dish improves in flavor when prepared in advance, so there's no last-minute angst. At serving time, you simply reheat the veal in its sauce, cook the pasta, and arrange both on a platter.

Serves 6

COST: Moderate

PREP TIME: 25 minutes

START-TO-FINISH TIME: About 3 hours

6 veal shanks, cut about 1 to 1¼ in/
   2.5 to 3 cm thick (4 lb/1.8 kg total)
Kosher salt
4 tbsp/60 ml olive oil
4 cups/500 g chopped onion
4 medium carrots, peeled and cut on the
   diagonal into slices ½ in/12 mm thick
4 medium garlic cloves, smashed and peeled
Two 28-oz/795-g cans Italian-style tomatoes,
   drained and coarsely chopped
4 tsp dried sage leaves, crumbled
   (not powdered sage)
2 bay leaves, broken in half
3 cups/720 ml reduced-sodium chicken broth
1 cup/240 ml dry red wine
1 to 1¼ lb/455 to 570 g fresh or
   dried fettuccine
1½ tbsp unsalted butter
2 tbsp minced flat-leaf parsley, for garnish

1. Arrange a rack at center position and preheat the oven to 350°F/180°C/gas 4.

2. Pat the veal shanks dry and season generously with salt on both sides. Heat the oil in an extra-large, deep-sided frying pan (with a lid) over medium-high heat. (If you don't have a frying pan large enough to fit all of the veal shanks and then the vegetables, use a large, flameproof roasting pan/tray.) When the oil is hot, add the veal and brown well, for 4 minutes per side. Remove the veal to a platter. Add the onions, carrots, and garlic to the pan. Sauté the vegetables, stirring frequently, for 5 minutes. Return the veal to the pan along with any juices that have collected on the platter. Add the tomatoes, sage, bay leaves, 2 tsp salt, broth, and wine.

3. Bring this mixture to a simmer, then cover and place it in the oven. (If using a roasting pan/tray, cover tightly with a double thickness of foil.) Roast until the meat is very tender, for about 2 hours. (The veal can be prepared 2 days ahead; cool, cover, and refrigerate. Reheat covered in a 350°F/180°C/gas 4 preheated oven until hot, for about 25 minutes.)

continued...

4. When the veal has finished roasting, return the frying pan with the shanks to the stovetop and set over medium-high heat. Cook, uncovered, until the liquids have reduced and thickened slightly, for 5 to 10 minutes or longer. Cover to keep warm while you prepare the pasta.

5. Cook the fettuccine in a large pot of boiling salted water until it is tender, according to the package directions, usually for about 5 minutes for fresh or 12 minutes for dried. Drain, toss with butter, and season with salt.

6. To serve, mound the pasta on a platter and top with veal shanks. Nap both the veal and pasta with sauce and sprinkle with parsley.

SIDES: A spinach or arugula/rocket salad tossed in lemon juice and olive oil and a loaf of ciabatta for sopping up the delicious sauce are all you need.

LEFTOVER TIP: Any veal and pasta that remains can be quickly reheated in a microwave or in a frying pan set over medium heat on the stove.

POULTRY

Chicken, Turkey, and More—
Old Favorites, Even Better

Whether it's the diminutive Cornish hen fit for a single diner or a plump turkey for fifteen-plus people, roasted poultry is easy to prepare and irresistible. With a little bit of care, you can transform whole birds as well as individual pieces into lusciously brown, succulent, and tender dishes.

The most important thing to remember is that poultry needs to be kept moist as it roasts so that it doesn't lose its natural juices. That's why so many of the recipes in this chapter call for brushing birds with butter or oil or even wrapping them in bacon before they go into the oven. Basting birds with additional butter or with liquids such as wine and broth as they cook will also ensure that they don't end up with parched skin. Finally, poultry needs to be fully cooked (no medium-rare here!), and the best test for doneness is to plunge an instant-read thermometer into the thickest part of a thigh and look for 170 to 180°F/77 to 82°C.

Every culture seems to have a favorite recipe for chicken or some other poultry, and you'll find recipes with flavors from around the globe on the following pages. Bistro Roast Chicken with Garlic, Onions, and Herbs pays homage to the French, who know how to roast chickens to perfection. Chicken Quarters Roasted with Lemons and Green Olives has Greek roots, while a Turkey Breast with Cremini, Porcini, and Pancetta Stuffing is redolent of the Italian pantry.

Whatever the occasion, you'll find a recipe for a glorious roasted bird in this chapter. For a simple family meal, try the quick Chicken Breasts Stuffed with Figs, Prosciutto, and Gorgonzola. With just a little more time, you can dazzle your clan with the Chipotle-Rubbed Turkey Breast with Fresh Corn Salsa. For Thanksgiving or Christmas celebrations, Golden Cider-Roasted Turkey and "Never Fail" Roast Turkey with Shallot Pan Gravy are winners. Enjoy!

Bistro Roast Chicken with Garlic, Onions, and Herbs

Because all of us succumb to those little supermarket rotisserie chickens from time to time, we need to be reminded of just how good a homemade version can be. This bistro-style roast chicken, a big bird that you slather with flavorful butter and baste frequently, is not likely to disappoint. A trinity of herbs–parsley, rosemary, and thyme–and some crushed fennel seeds season the butter, which is used to baste the chicken, as well as the onion wedges and garlic cloves that roast along with it. To gild the lily (or the bird in this case!), there's a rich sauce prepared with the pan drippings.

Serves 6

COST: Inexpensive

PREP TIME: 35 minutes

START-TO-FINISH TIME:
2 hours, 35 minutes,
including resting time
for the chicken

8 tbsp/115 g unsalted butter,
  at room temperature

1 tbsp minced flat-leaf parsley, plus 3 sprigs

1 tbsp minced fresh rosemary, plus 3 sprigs

1 tbsp minced fresh thyme, plus 3 sprigs

¼ tsp fennel seeds, crushed

Kosher salt

1 roasting chicken, 6 to 7 lb/2.7 to 3.2 kg,
  with neck and giblets removed and discarded
  or saved for another use

Freshly ground black pepper

3 medium onions, peeled and quartered
  lengthwise without removing root ends

14 medium garlic cloves, peeled

1 cup/240 ml reduced-sodium chicken broth

½ cup/120 ml dry white wine

1½ tbsp all-purpose flour/plain flour

1. Combine the butter, minced parsley, minced rosemary, minced thyme, fennel seeds, and ½ tsp salt in a bowl. Remove 1 tbsp of this mixture and reserve for the sauce. (The butter can be made 1 day ahead; cover and refrigerate. Bring to room temperature 30 minutes or longer to soften before using.)

2. Arrange a rack at lower position and preheat the oven to 400°F/200°C/gas 6.

3. Rinse the chicken and pat dry. Season the cavity with salt and pepper, then fill it with the parsley, rosemary, and thyme sprigs. Slide your fingers under the skin of the breast and the upper part of the legs to loosen. Spread 3 tbsp of the herb butter under the skin covering the breast and upper leg meat.

4. Place the chicken on an adjustable rack in a large, flame-proof roasting pan/tray. Tie the legs together so that the chicken will hold its shape. Scatter the onion wedges around the chicken; brush the chicken skin and dot the onions with 2 tbsp of the herb butter. Sprinkle with salt and pepper.

5. Roast the bird for 30 minutes, then remove the pan and stir the onions. Scatter the garlic cloves around the chicken. Brush the chicken, onions, and garlic with 1 tbsp of the herb butter.

6. Roast the chicken and vegetables for 30 minutes more. Brush the remaining herb butter over the chicken and vegetables.

7. Continue to roast until the chicken is golden and the juices run clear when the thickest part of the thigh is pierced with a knife, for about 30 minutes longer. A thermometer inserted into the thickest part of the thigh should register 175 to 180°F/80 to 82°C.

8. Lift the chicken with a long-handled wooden spoon and tilt slightly, emptying any juice from the cavity into the pan. Transfer the chicken to a platter and surround with the onions and garlic. Tent loosely with foil and let rest for 15 minutes while you prepare the sauce.

9. Pour the pan juices into a large glass measuring cup; spoon off any fat from the top and discard. Set the roasting pan/tray over 1 or 2 burners at medium-high heat. Add the broth and wine and, with a wire whisk, scrape up any browned bits into the liquids. Add the pan juices from the measuring cup and bring the mixture to a simmer. Blend the reserved tablespoon of herb butter and the flour in a small bowl to make a smooth paste. Whisk the paste into the liquids and simmer the sauce until slightly thickened, for 3 to 4 minutes. Season with salt and pepper.

10. Serve the chicken with a bowl of the sauce.

SIDES: Best-Ever Mashed Potatoes, either the basic recipe or the Buttermilk–Country Mustard variation (page 138), and 5-Minute Roasted Sugar Snap Peas (page 149) would make fine side dishes.

LEFTOVER TIPS: There are countless ways to use leftover Bistro Roast Chicken. You can cut it into chunks and use it in pot pies, adding any leftover sauce to the filling. For a great salad, combine julienned slices of the chicken, sliced Granny Smith apples, and baby spinach, then toss in a mustard vinaigrette. Garnish with some crumbled bacon and shaved white cheddar.

Chicken Breasts Stuffed with Figs, Prosciutto, and Gorgonzola

A celestial trio of Italian ingredients—dried figs, sliced prosciutto, and creamy Gorgonzola— makes an irresistible filling for boneless chicken breasts. Once stuffed and skewered, the breasts are pan-seared, then quickly roasted until golden brown. A glaze made with honey and balsamic vinegar gives the chicken a polished look and complements the distinctive flavors of the stuffing.

Serves 4

COST: Moderate

PREP TIME: 15 minutes

START-TO-FINISH TIME: 40 minutes

MATERIALS: Short wooden skewers or sturdy toothpicks, soaked in water for 30 minutes

4 large, boneless skinless chicken breast halves, 7 to 8 oz/200 to 225 g each

Kosher salt

Freshly ground black pepper

8 thin slices prosciutto (4 oz/120 g)

One 5-oz/145-g wedge Gorgonzola, crumbled

½ cup/80 g thinly sliced dried figs, preferably Black Mission

1½ tbsp olive oil

½ cup/120 ml balsamic vinegar

¼ cup/60 ml honey

2 tbsp minced flat-leaf parsley

Fleur de sel

1. Using a very sharp knife held parallel to the work surface, make a horizontal slit through a chicken breast, stopping just short of cutting it in half, and open the breast up like a book. Repeat with the remaining breasts. Cover the breasts with plastic wrap/cling film and pound until they're ¼ in/ 6 mm thick, then salt and pepper them.

2. Cover half of each breast with 2 prosciutto slices, and then divide the cheese evenly over the prosciutto. Divide the figs evenly and place over the cheese on the breasts. Close each breast and secure each with 2 or 3 wooden skewers. Salt and pepper the breasts on both sides. (The chicken breasts can be prepared 2 hours ahead; cover and refrigerate.)

3. Arrange a rack at center position and preheat the oven to 400°F/200°C/gas 6.

4. Heat the oil in a large, heavy, ovenproof frying pan set over medium heat. When hot, add the breasts and cook for 1 minute per side. Place the pan in the oven and roast until the chicken is very tender and the juices run clear when pierced with a knife, for 12 to 15 minutes, turning once after 6 minutes.

5. Using oven mitts, remove the frying pan from the oven and transfer the breasts to a carving board. Tent them loosely with foil.

6. Add the balsamic vinegar and honey to the frying pan and, again using mitts, since the handle will be quite hot, place the pan over high heat. Cook, stirring often, until the mixture has reduced to ½ cup/120 ml, for about 5 minutes.

7. To serve, use a dish/tea towel or mitts to remove the skewers or toothpicks and cut each breast crosswise on the diagonal into slices 1 in/2.5 cm thick. Arrange the slices on a platter, slightly overlapping. Drizzle with some sauce and garnish with a sprinkle of parsley and fleur de sel.

SIDES: Serve this chicken with buttered linguine or orzo and with tender green beans sprinkled with toasted pine nuts.

LEFTOVER TIP. For lunch or a light supper, garnish a mixed greens salad tossed in a balsamic vinaigrette with cold slices of the chicken and enjoy with some crusty peasant bread.

Chicken Quarters Roasted with Lemons and Green Olives

Many cooks overlook dark-fleshed thighs and legs in favor of their white-meat counterparts, breasts and wings. The truth is that thighs and legs are both moist and flavorful and can easily take center stage. In the following dish, chicken quarters (both legs and thighs) are roasted slowly in an aromatic mix of green olives, lemon, and white wine until they are golden brown, juicy, and tender. For serving, the chicken is showered with crumbled feta.

Serves 6

COST: Inexpensive

PREP TIME: 30 minutes

START-TO-FINISH TIME: about 1 hour, 45 minutes

3 large, thick-skinned lemons

6 chicken leg-and-thigh quarters with skin left on, about 3½ lb/1.6 kg total (see market note, page 98)

Kosher salt

Freshly ground black pepper

3 to 4 tbsp/45 to 60 ml olive oil

¾ cup/75 g chopped shallots (2 to 3 large shallots)

6 tbsp/12 g minced flat-leaf parsley

4 tsp minced garlic

2 tsp dried oregano

1¼ cups/300 ml dry white wine

1 cup/175 g green Mediterranean olives, pitted or unpitted (see market note, page 98)

¾ to 1 cup/180 to 240 ml chicken broth

½ cup/80 g crumbled feta cheese

1. Arrange a rack at center position and preheat the oven to 375°F/190°C/gas 5.

2. Zest 2 of the lemons to yield 2 tbsp zest, and juice to yield ¼ cup/60 ml juice. Cut the third lemon into 6 wedges for the garnish.

3. Pat the chicken quarters dry with paper towels/absorbent paper. Trim and discard any excess fat or dangling skin. Salt and pepper the chicken generously on both sides. Place an extra-large ovenproof frying pan (with a lid; see cooking tip) over medium-high heat with enough oil to coat the bottom (3 to 4 tbsp). When the oil is very hot but not smoking, add the chicken pieces in a single layer. Brown well on all sides, turning several times, for about 12 to 15 minutes. Remove the pan from the heat and transfer the chicken to a side dish. Reserve 4 tbsp/60 ml of the oil in the frying pan and discard the rest (or add more oil to make 4 tbsp/60 ml if necessary).

4. Return the pan to the stove over low heat. Add the shallots and cook, stirring, until just softened but not browned, for 1 to 2 minutes. Add half of the parsley, the garlic, and the oregano, and cook for 1 minute. Stir in the lemon zest and juice, wine, and olives, and then return the chicken to the pan.

continued...

5. Bring the mixture to a simmer, then cover the frying pan and place it in the oven. Roast until the chicken is very tender when pierced with a knife, for 45 to 50 minutes, then remove the lid and roast for 5 to 10 minutes longer to let the juices reduce slightly. Watch carefully so that the juices do not evaporate completely.

6. Remove the chicken to a platter; tent loosely with foil and set aside. Add ¾ cup/180 ml broth to the pan and heat until it is warm. The mixture should have a very thin, sauce-like consistency. If too thick, add an additional ¼ cup/60 ml broth. (The chicken can be prepared 1 day ahead; cool, cover, and refrigerate. Reheat, covered, in a 350°F/180°C/gas 4 oven until hot, 15 minutes or longer, adding extra broth if needed.)

7. To serve, pour the juices in the pan over the chicken. Sprinkle with feta cheese and with the remaining parsley, and garnish with the lemon wedges.

SIDES: This chicken, which is definitely Mediterranean in character, would be delicious served with Zucchini and Tomato Gratin (page 142) and with a bowl of buttered couscous or orzo.

LEFTOVER TIP: Rewarm leftover chicken and, for a great lunch or light supper, serve it with a mixed greens salad dressed in lemon and olive oil. Serve with a basket of toasted pitas.

MARKET NOTES: If you can't find whole chicken legs (that is, the leg and thigh attached together), you can use six thighs and six legs.

Picholine or Lucques olives are good green French olives that work well in this recipe.

COOKING TIP: If you do not have an extra-large frying pan, you can use a flameproof roasting pan/tray covered with a double thickness of foil.

Golden Cider-Roasted Turkey

As this turkey roasts to a rich golden brown, it fills the kitchen with the enticing aroma of apples and leeks, which roast along with it. Cider, used to baste the bird and also in the scrumptious sauce, adds a fresh, fruity accent to this roasted fowl. The recipe calls for a 14-lb/6.3-kg bird, perfect for serving eight with leftovers.

Serves 8

COST: Moderate

PREP TIME: 25 minutes

START-TO-FINISH TIME:
4 hours, 10 minutes,
including resting time
for the turkey

MATERIALS:
Kitchen twine

One 13- to14-lb/5.9- to 6.3-kg turkey, rinsed
   and patted dry
Kosher salt
Freshly ground black pepper
2 cups/160 g chopped leeks, white and light
   green parts only (3 to 4 leeks)
2 small Granny Smith apples, peeled, cored,
   and cut into ½-in/12-mm dice
4 fresh sage sprigs, plus extra sprigs
   for garnish
4 fresh thyme sprigs, plus extra sprigs
   for garnish
12 tbsp/170 g unsalted butter,
   at room temperature
1 tbsp dried sage leaves
1 tbsp dried thyme leaves
2½ cups/600 ml fresh apple cider
1¼ cups/300 ml dry white wine
2 to 3 tbsp flour

1. Arrange a rack at center position and preheat the oven to 325°F/165°C/gas 3.

2. Season the cavity of the turkey generously with salt and pepper. Combine the leeks and apples in a medium bowl, and place 1 cup/100 g of this mixture in the cavity along with 4 sage and 4 thyme sprigs.

3. In a medium bowl, mix together the butter, dried sage, dried thyme, 1½ tsp salt, and 1 tsp pepper until well blended. Reserve 2 tbsp of this butter for the sauce and set aside. Use 4 tbsp/55 g of the remaining herb butter and rub it over the surface of the turkey. Truss the turkey: Use a long piece of kitchen twine and tie the legs together, slightly overlapping, then bring the string around the sides of the bird, pulling the wings toward the body, and tie the twine to secure (see cooking tip).

4. Place the turkey on a rack set in a large flameproof roasting pan/tray. Spread the remaining leeks and apples on the bottom of the pan. Combine the cider and white wine and reserve 1½ cups/360 ml of this mixture for the sauce; pour ⅓ cup/75 ml of the remaining cider mixture over the turkey.

5. Roast the turkey until golden brown and a thermometer inserted into the thickest part of the thigh registers 180°F/82°C, basting every 30 minutes with ⅓ cup/75 ml of the cider mixture and 1 tbsp of the herb butter, for about

continued...

3 hours and 10 minutes or longer. Watch carefully and if the turkey begins to brown too much, cover it loosely with foil. When done, remove the turkey to a platter and tent it loosely with foil. Let rest for 30 minutes while you prepare the sauce.

6. Drain the liquids from the roasting pan/tray into a bowl, pressing down hard on the roasted leeks and apples to release all the juices; discard the solids. Skim off and discard any fat from the drippings and return the drained juices to the pan. Add the reserved cider mixture and any leftover cider mixture from basting to the pan and place it over 2 burners set on medium-high heat. Using a whisk, scrape up any brown bits on the bottom of pan into the liquids. Cook, whisking often, until the liquids have reduced by about a third, for 5 minutes.

7. Combine the reserved 2 tbsp herb butter and any butter left over from basting with 2 tbsp of flour and blend with a fork to make a paste (if you want the sauce to be thicker, increase the flour to 3 tbsp). Whisk the butter-flour mixture into the pan a little at a time until the sauce thickens and coats the back of a spoon, for 5 to 6 minutes. Season the sauce with salt if needed and transfer it to a serving bowl.

8. To serve, remove and discard the twine and the ingredients from the cavity. Garnish the turkey with bouquets of sage and thyme sprigs. Pass the sauce on the side.

SIDES: Sourdough Dressing with Roasted Root Vegetables (page 158) or Best-Ever Mashed Potatoes Buttermilk–Country Mustard variation (page 138), Green Beans with Caramelized Shallots (page 151), and Cranberry and Dried Cherry Chutney (page 165) would make mouthwatering accompaniments.

LEFTOVER TIP: Use this leftover turkey, with its slight hint of sweetness, for sandwiches made with whole-wheat bread, lots of Dijon mustard, farmhouse cheddar, and a good dollop of cranberry chutney or sauce.

COOKING TIP: The reason a turkey is trussed is to help it keep its shape and ensure that it roasts evenly.

"Never Fail" Roast Turkey with Shallot Pan Gravy

This is one of my favorite recipes for roasting a big, plump turkey. As the name implies, it's always a winner. The secret to its success is twofold. First, an herb butter is patted under the skin over the breast area, ensuring that this part of the turkey, which cooks the quickest, stays moist. Then, during the roasting process, the turkey is basted frequently with broth and pan juices to keep it from drying out. Shallots are roasted along with the bird, and then incorporated into the delectable pan gravy.

Serves 10 to 12

COST: Moderate

PREP TIME: 45 minutes

START-TO-FINISH TIME:
4 hours, 15 minutes,
including resting time
for the turkey

MATERIALS:
Kitchen twine

¾ cup/170 g unsalted butter,
  at room temperature
3 tbsp minced flat-leaf parsley,
  plus 3 whole sprigs
2 tbsp minced fresh sage, plus 3 whole sprigs
2 tbsp minced fresh thyme, plus 3 whole sprigs
Kosher salt
Freshly ground black pepper
1 turkey, 15 to 16 lb/6.8 to 7.2 kg,
  rinsed and patted dry
1½ lb/680 g shallots, peeled and halved
  lengthwise
3 cups/720 ml reduced-sodium chicken broth,
  plus more as needed
1 cup/240 ml dry white wine
2 tbsp flour
1 bunch each flat-leaf parsley, sage, and
  thyme for garnish (optional)

1. Mix together the butter, minced parsley, minced sage, minced thyme, ¾ tsp salt and ½ tsp pepper in a medium bowl. (The butter can be prepared 1 day ahead. Cover and refrigerate. Bring to room temperature before using.)

2. Arrange a rack at the lower position of the oven and preheat the oven to 350°F/180°C/gas 4.

3. Salt and pepper the cavity of the turkey generously. Place the parsley, sage, and thyme sprigs and 4 shallot halves in the cavity. Pat the turkey skin dry with paper towels/absorbent paper. Starting at the neck end of the turkey, carefully slide your hand between the skin and the breast meat to loosen the skin. Spread 3 tbsp of the herb butter over the breast meat under the skin. Truss the turkey: Use a long piece of kitchen twine and tie the legs together, slightly overlapping, then bring the twine around the sides of the bird, pulling the wings toward the body, and tie the twine to secure (see cooking tip, page 100).

4. Place the turkey on a rack set in a large flameproof roasting pan/tray. Rub 4 tbsp/55 g of the herb butter all over the surface of the turkey. Cover the breast area with foil. Scatter the remaining shallots in the pan to roast along with the turkey.

5. Roast the turkey for 2 hours, basting with ½ cup/120 ml broth every 30 minutes. Remove the foil and continue to roast the turkey until golden brown and a thermometer inserted into the thickest part of the thigh registers

180°F/82°C, basting with pan juices every 20 minutes, for about 1 hour more. Total roasting time will be about 3 hours. Transfer the turkey to a platter. Brush with 1 tbsp of the herb butter and tent loosely with foil. Let rest for 30 minutes.

6. With a slotted spoon, transfer the shallots from the roasting pan/tray to a plate. Pour the pan juices into a medium bowl; spoon off and discard any fat. Add the wine and the remaining 1 cup/240 ml chicken broth to the roasting pan/tray. Set the pan over 2 burners on medium-high heat and bring the mixture to a boil, scraping up any browned bits. Continue to boil until reduced by half, for about 3 minutes. Pour into a large glass measuring cup, and add the degreased pan juices. If necessary, add enough broth to equal 3 cups/720 ml liquid.

7. Blend the flour into the remaining herb butter. Pour the broth mixture into a heavy, medium saucepan set over medium-high heat and bring it to a boil. Gradually whisk in the butter-flour mixture and add any accumulated juices from the turkey platter. Cook, whisking occasionally, until the gravy thickens enough to coat a spoon lightly, for 5 to 6 minutes. Add the shallots to the gravy and simmer for 1 minute, then season with salt and pepper. Transfer the gravy to a serving bowl.

8. If desired, garnish the turkey platter with several mixed bouquets of parsley, sage, and thyme before serving. Pass the gravy on the side.

SIDES: Sourdough Dressing with Roasted Root Vegetables (page 158), Cranberry and Dried Cherry Chutney (page 165), Butternut Squash with Walnut–Goat Cheese Crumble (page 144), and Honey-Glazed Carrots and Parsnips (page 145) would make scrumptious trimmings.

LEFTOVER TIPS: In addition to classic turkey sandwiches, use leftover turkey in quesadillas paired with white cheddar and sliced apples, or use in place of pastrami for turkey Reubens.

Chipotle-Rubbed Turkey Breast with Fresh Corn Salsa

Boned turkey breasts are reasonably priced and unbelievably versatile, and yet I don't think many cooks take advantage of this delicious cut. Since my local supermarket often runs specials on turkey breasts, I've learned to use them creatively. In the following recipe, a boned breast is rubbed with a smoky chili mix, and then wrapped in bacon strips. As the breast roasts, the bacon bastes the meat and keeps it moist. For serving, the beautiful white turkey slices are drizzled with pan juices and topped with a homemade corn salsa.

Serves 4 to 6

COST: Moderate

PREP TIME: 40 minutes, including making the salsa

START-TO-FINISH TIME: 2 hours, 10 minutes, including resting time for the turkey

MATERIALS: Kitchen twine

One 2-lb/910-g boneless turkey breast half, skin and any excess fat removed
1½ tsp chipotle chili powder
1½ tsp ground cumin
Kosher salt
1½ tbsp olive oil
10 slices bacon/streaky bacon
½ cup/120 ml chicken broth
1 tsp fresh lime juice
1½ tbsp minced cilantro/fresh coriander
Fresh Corn Salsa (page 168; see cooking tip)

1. Arrange a rack at center position and preheat the oven to 375°F/190°C/gas 5.

2. Place the turkey breast on a work surface. If it has been rolled and tied, untie it. In a small bowl, mix together the chili powder, cumin, and ¾ teaspoon salt. Rub half of this mixture over the inside surface, turn the breast over, and rub the remaining mixture over the other side. Roll the breast tightly into a cylinder (about 9 in/23 cm long and 3½ in/9 cm in diameter) and tie at 1-in/2.5-cm intervals with twine.

3. Heat the oil in a large, heavy frying pan over medium-high heat. When hot, add the turkey breast and brown on all sides, for 4 to 5 minutes. Remove the turkey breast from the frying pan and let it cool for 5 minutes.

4. On a clean work surface, lay the bacon slices, slightly overlapping, side by side. Place the turkey breast seam-side up in the center and wrap the bacon slices around the breast so that they overlap. Transfer the breast (with overlapping-bacon–side down) to a rack set in a large flameproof roasting pan/tray. (The turkey breast can be prepared 6 hours ahead; cover the pan with plastic wrap/cling film and refrigerate. Bring to room temperature for 30 minutes before roasting.)

5. Roast the breast until a thermometer inserted into the center registers 170°F/77°C, for about 1 hour, 15 minutes, or longer. Remove the breast from the pan and let it rest for 15 minutes.

6. Skim off and discard any fat in the pan. Place the pan over medium heat and add the broth. Whisk constantly, scraping up any browned bits on the bottom of the pan into the liquids. Whisk in the lime juice and season with salt if needed. The sauce will be very thin, but flavorful.

7. To serve, cut the turkey breast through the bacon (which will be completely cooked) into slices ½ in/12 mm thick, carefully discarding the strings as you slice. Arrange the slices slightly overlapping on a platter and drizzle with the pan sauce. Sprinkle with cilantro/fresh coriander and serve with a bowl of the salsa.

SIDES: Serve this turkey with tender green beans sprinkled with sea salt and with a salad of torn romaine/Cos lettuce and avocados tossed in a dressing of lime and olive oil.

LEFTOVER TIP: This turkey is great in a sandwich. Use bread slices and add sliced tomatoes, a squeeze of lime juice, and some crispy lettuce if you like.

COOKING TIP: In place of Fresh Corn Salsa, you could serve this turkey breast with Chunky Guacamole Salsa (page 170).

Turkey Breast with Cremini, Porcini, and Pancetta Stuffing

When you want to serve turkey elegantly and on a small scale, try this spectacular boned and stuffed breast. Although it will require more than an hour of your time to assemble the stuffing and to prepare the breast, both of these tasks can be done a day ahead. The breast roasts to a beautiful golden brown in about 45 minutes, far less time than a big bird would need. When carved, the slices are striking, with the dark, rich mushroom stuffing set against the luminous white turkey meat.

Serves 4 to 6

COST: Moderate

PREP TIME: 1 hour, 30 minutes, including 10 minutes to butterfly the breast if necessary

START-TO-FINISH TIME: 2 hours, 45 minutes

MATERIALS: Kitchen twine

Short metal skewers, or wooden skewers that have been soaked in water for 30 minutes (see market note, page 108)

Stuffing
¾ oz/20 g dried porcini mushrooms

4 oz/115 g sliced pancetta, coarsely chopped

2 tbsp vegetable oil

6 oz/170 g brown mushrooms, such as cremini, chopped

½ cup/65 g finely chopped onion

¼ cup/8 g finely minced flat-leaf parsley

1 tbsp minced fresh rosemary

½ tsp fennel seeds, crushed

Kosher salt

Freshly ground black pepper

2 cups/110 g fresh bread crumbs (see cooking tip, page 49)

Turkey
1 boneless turkey breast half, about 2 ¾ lb/ 1.25 kg, with skin left on, butterflied (see cooking tip, page 108)

Kosher salt

Freshly ground black pepper

2 tbsp vegetable oil

2 cups/480 ml reduced-sodium chicken broth, plus more if needed

4 tbsp/55 g unsalted butter, at room temperature, plus more if needed

2 tbsp flour

¼ cup/60 ml dry white wine

Several long sprigs parsley and rosemary for garnish

FOR THE STUFFING:

1. Put the porcini in a medium bowl and cover with 1 cup boiling water. Let stand until softened, for about 20 minutes. Over a medium bowl, strain the mushrooms with a fine strainer, pressing down to release as much liquid as possible. Chop the mushrooms; reserve the mushrooms and the strained liquid separately.

2. Place a large, heavy frying pan over medium heat. When hot, add the pancetta and sauté, stirring, until crisp, for 6 to 8 minutes. With a slotted spoon, transfer to paper towels/absorbent paper to drain. Add the oil to the drippings in the pan and, when hot, add the brown mushrooms and onion. Sauté, stirring, until the mushrooms start to brown and no liquid remains, for 6 minutes or more. Remove the pan from the heat and stir in the pancetta, chopped porcini, parsley, rosemary, fennel seeds, ¾ tsp salt, ½ tsp pepper, and bread crumbs. Mix well and season with additional salt and pepper if needed. Stir in 3 tbsp of the reserved porcini mushroom liquid or just enough to moisten but not soak the bread crumbs. Cool to room temperature.

FOR THE TURKEY:

1. Cover the butterflied breast with a sheet of plastic wrap/cling film and, using a meat pounder or rolling pin, pound the meat into a ½-in/12-mm-thick rectangle (about 14 by 10 in/35.5 by 25 cm). Remove the plastic wrap/cling film and season the breast with salt and pepper.

2. Pat the stuffing evenly over the turkey breast, leaving a 1-in/2.5-cm border on all sides. Sprinkle with additional porcini mushroom liquid if dry. Starting at a long end, roll into a cylinder and tie at 1-in/2.5-cm intervals. Close the ends of the roast with skewers. (The turkey can be prepared 4 hours ahead; cover and refrigerate.)

3. Arrange a rack at center position and preheat the oven to 375°F/190°C/gas 5.

4. Heat the oil in a large, flameproof roasting pan/tray set over 1 or 2 burners on medium heat. When hot, add the breast and brown on all sides, for 6 to 8 minutes.

5. Pour ⅓ cup/75 ml chicken broth over the roast in the pan and brush with 1 tbsp butter. Cover the pan tightly with foil. Roast for 30 minutes, basting the roast 2 more times with ⅓ cup/75 ml broth and with 1 tbsp butter. (Be careful to use mitts so that you do not burn yourself when you

continued...

remove the foil to baste the bird.) Remove the foil and continue to roast until the turkey is evenly browned and an instant-read thermometer registers 170°F/77°C when inserted into center of the roast, basting occasionally with broth and butter, for about 15 minutes longer. Total roasting time will be about 45 minutes. Transfer the turkey to a carving board and tent with foil. Let rest for 15 minutes while you make the sauce.

6. Pour the pan juices into a glass measuring cup. Add additional broth if needed to measure 1¼ cups/300 ml liquid. In a small bowl, blend 2 tbsp of butter with flour to form a paste.

7. Place the roasting pan over medium-high heat and add 1¼ cups/300 ml pan juices, any remaining porcini mushroom liquid, any extra butter, and the wine. Cook for 5 minutes, scraping up any brown bits on the bottom of the pan with a whisk. A little at a time, whisk in the butter-flour mixture. Continue to whisk until the sauce thickens slightly, for about 3 minutes more. Season with salt and pepper.

8. To serve, remove the strings and skewers. Cut the breast into ½-in-/12-mm-thick slices and arrange them overlapping on a platter. Garnish with bouquets of parsley and rosemary sprigs. Pass the sauce separately.

SIDES: Best-Ever Mashed Potatoes (page 138), Honey-Glazed Carrots and Parsnips (page 145), and Cranberry and Dried Cherry Chutney (page 165) would make delicious sides.

LEFTOVER TIP: Extra sliced turkey is delectable reheated and napped with leftover sauce, and the slices are equally good served at room temperature (without sauce) accompanied by a green salad tossed in a balsamic dressing.

MARKET NOTE: You can use metal turkey-lacing pins (available at supermarkets) in place of skewers to secure the ends of the roast.

COOKING TIP: For this recipe, a boneless turkey breast half is double butterflied: The breast is split lengthwise down the center and opened, then each side is slit, this time horizontally, and opened. This will give you a nice rectangular piece. If you are on good terms with your butcher, smile and ask him or her to do this for you. If not, just follow the directions below.

Place the breast on a work surface, skin-side down, with the pointed, narrow end toward you. (If there is a tender on the underside of the breast, remove and save it for another use.) With a sharp knife, starting at the upper, thicker end of the breast, cut a lengthwise slit down the center of the breast, being careful not to cut all the way through and stopping 1 in/2.5 cm from the pointed narrow end. With the knife held horizontal to the work surface, slice about one-half to two-thirds of the way through the center of each side of the breast and open each side up like a book.

Cornish Hens with Fennel and Fingerlings

What could be more convenient than a one-pan roasted meal? Halved Cornish hens are quickly browned, then set atop sautéed fennel and fingerling potatoes. Both the birds and the vegetables are seasoned with herbes de Provence before they go into the oven. A simple pan sauce made with white wine and butter is a fine finishing touch. Mounded on a platter and surrounded by the fennel and potatoes, the hens make a striking appearance.

Serves 4, with a half hen per serving

COST: Moderate

PREP TIME: 25 minutes

START-TO-FINISH TIME: 1 hour, 30 minutes

2 medium fennel bulbs (1½ to 2 lb/680 to 910 g total)

2 Cornish hens, each about 1½ lb/680 g, split and patted dry (see cooking tip, page 111)

1½ tbsp herbes de Provence (see market note, page 111)

1½ tsp kosher salt

1 tsp freshly ground black pepper

8 tbsp/120 ml olive oil, plus more as needed

1 lb/455 g fingerling potatoes, scrubbed but not peeled, halved lengthwise

½ cup/120 ml dry white wine

2 tbsp unsalted butter, at room temperature

1. Arrange a rack at center position and preheat the oven to 400°F/200°C/gas 6.

2. Trim the lacy stems from the fennel bulbs; place the stems in a glass of water and reserve for the garnish. Halve the fennel bulbs and cut out and discard the tough triangular cores. Cut lengthwise into ½-in/12-mm julienne strips.

3. Rinse the split birds and pat dry with paper towels/absorbent paper. In a small bowl, combine the herbes de Provence, salt, and pepper. Rub half of this mixture on both sides of the Cornish hens.

4. In a large, heavy, flameproof roasting pan/tray set over 1 or 2 burners on medium-high heat, heat 5 tbsp/75 ml of the olive oil until hot. Add the Cornish hens, cut-side down, and cook, turning several times, until browned on all sides, for 8 to 10 minutes. Remove to a platter.

5. Add an additional 2 tbsp of the olive oil and heat until hot. Add the fennel and potatoes and sauté, turning, just until lightly browned, for about 5 minutes. If necessary, add more oil. Stir in the remaining herbes de Provence mixture. Place the pan in the oven and roast the vegetables for 15 minutes.

continued...

6. Remove the pan from the oven, and arrange the hens, cut-side down, on top of the vegetables. Brush the hens with the remaining tablespoon of olive oil. Return the pan to the oven and roast for 10 minutes. Reduce the temperature to 350°F/180°C/gas 4 and continue to roast until the Cornish hens have juices that run clear when the thighs are pierced with a sharp knife, for 20 to 25 minutes longer.

7. Transfer the hens and vegetables to a platter and cover loosely with foil. Place the roasting pan/tray over a burner set on medium-high heat. Add the wine and whisk well to loosen any brown bits on the bottom of the pan. Bring the mixture to a simmer, then whisk in the butter. Cook, whisking, until the sauce thickens slightly, for about 2 minutes.

8. To serve, pour the sauce over the hens and garnish the platter with a few of the lacy fennel stems.

SIDES: This dish could be served as is, since there are two vegetables roasted with the hens. However, if you want to add a splash of color, include Honey-Glazed Carrots and Parsnips (page 145).

LEFTOVER TIP: If, by chance, you have potatoes and/or fennel left over, you could use them along with a few tablespoons of grated Gruyère or cheddar as a filling for an omelet. Just add a green salad and you'll have another meal.

MARKET NOTE: Herbes de Provence, a mixture of Provencal herbs that often includes basil, rosemary, sage, thyme, fennel seed, lavender, marjoram, and summer savory, is available in many supermarkets.

COOKING TIP: Use kitchen shears or a heavy, sharp knife to cut the birds in half.

Cornish Hens with Orange-Cherry Sauce

Split into halves for easy handling, then brushed with melted butter scented with orange, these little birds are roasted until golden brown and tender to the bone. A mixture of chicken broth and orange juice concentrate is used to baste the hens as they roast, keeping them moist and infusing them with an assertive punch of citrus flavor. A delectable sauce prepared with the pan drippings and dried cherries is spooned over the birds for serving.

Serves 6, with a half hen per serving

COST: Moderate

PREP TIME: 20 minutes

START-TO-FINISH TIME: 1 hour, 10 minutes

1 cup/160 g dried cherries

3 Cornish hens, each about 1½ lb/680 g, split (see cooking tip, page 111)

Kosher salt

Freshly ground black pepper

4½ tbsp/62 g unsalted butter, melted and cooled slightly, plus more as needed

1 tbsp dried thyme leaves

2½ tsp grated orange zest

2 cups/480 ml reduced-sodium chicken broth

½ cup/120 ml frozen orange juice concentrate, defrosted

1 to 2 tsp cornstarch/cornflour

1 bunch fresh thyme, for garnish (optional)

1. Arrange a rack at center position and preheat the oven to 400°F/200°C/gas 6.

2. Place the cherries in a medium bowl, cover with hot water, and soak for 10 minutes. Drain and set aside.

3. Rinse the split birds and pat dry with paper towels/ absorbent paper. Place the hens, cut-side down, in a large, flameproof roasting pan/tray that will accommodate them in a single layer without crowding. Salt and pepper generously.

4. Mix together the melted butter, thyme, orange zest, 1 tsp salt, and 1 tsp pepper in a small bowl. Brush the birds with the butter and roast for 15 minutes. While the birds are roasting, whisk the chicken broth and orange juice concentrate together in a bowl and reserve 1 cup/240 ml of this mixture for the sauce.

5. After 15 minutes, reduce the oven temperature to 375°F/ 190°C/gas 5 and baste the birds with ⅓ cup/75 ml of the broth-orange juice mixture. Continue basting every 10 minutes with ⅓ cup/75 ml of the broth mixture until the hens are golden brown and their juices run clear when the thighs are pierced with a sharp knife, for about 30 minutes more. If the hens appear to be drying out, brush with more melted butter, or if the pan drippings start to burn, add more broth mixture to the pan.

6. Transfer the hens to a serving platter and cover loosely with foil.

7. Place the roasting pan/tray over 1 or 2 burners on medium heat and add the cherries and the reserved 1 cup/240 ml of broth mixture, plus any remaining broth used for basting. Whisk for 1 to 2 minutes, scraping up any brown bits on the bottom of the pan into the liquids. In a small bowl, whisk together 1 tsp cornstarch/cornflour with 1 tsp cold water, then whisk into the liquids in the pan. Continue whisking until the sauce thickens slightly and lightly coats the back of a spoon. If the sauce doesn't thicken within a minute, combine another teaspoon of cornstarch/cornflour and water and whisk into the pan. Season the sauce with salt if needed.

8. To serve, ladle the sauce over the hens. If desired, garnish the platter with several small clusters of fresh thyme.

SIDES: Serve these beautiful birds with Wild Rice with Roasted Grapes and Walnuts (page 155) and some pureed butternut squash, seasoned with honey.

LEFTOVER TIP: Reheat any remaining birds and sauce and serve over buttered noodles.

Honey-Roasted Duck with Sautéed Potatoes

Many people love to order roast duck in a restaurant, but wouldn't dream of preparing it at home. There's something elusive about how to cook this bird with the big frame and fairly small amount of flesh. When creating the following recipe, I asked talented chef Matt Sunderland for help to ensure that the duck would have nicely browned, crisp skin and flavorful meat beneath. To achieve the first, he suggested that I use a Chinese technique that calls for rinsing the bird in hot water and then letting it dry out overnight. To guarantee great flavor, he proposed honey, orange, and black pepper as seasonings. Since there is plenty of rich duck fat rendered during roasting, I saved some for sautéing diced potatoes to accompany the bird.

Serves 4

COST: Splurge

PREP TIME: 20 minutes

START-TO-FINISH TIME: About 24 hours, including 1 hour, 40 minutes for bringing the duck to room temperature, roasting it and letting it rest

---

1 duck, 5 to 5½ lb/2.3 to 2.5 kg, with giblets and neck removed from the cavity and discarded or saved for another use

¾ cup/180 ml honey

Kosher salt

Coarsely ground black pepper

1 large orange, cut into thin slices, plus 1 tbsp grated orange zest and 1 tbsp fresh orange juice

2 medium garlic cloves, crushed and peeled

1½ lb/680 g Yukon gold potatoes, peeled and cut into ¾-in/2-cm dice

1 bunch watercress

---

1. Trim and discard any pockets of fat from the cavity and any dangling pieces of fat and skin from the duck.

2. Use a clean, empty wine bottle and, holding the duck upright, slide the bottle into its cavity. Place the duck on the bottle in the sink and pour 3 to 4 cups/720 to 960 ml hot water over it. Repeat two more times. (This will help shrink the skin and make it crisper when roasted.)

3. Pat the duck dry with paper towels/absorbent paper and stand it (still on the wine bottle) in a large, shallow pan. Brush ¼ cup/60 ml of the honey over all surfaces of the duck and let it stand, uncovered, at room temperature to dry out completely, for 3 to 4 hours. Brush the duck with another ¼ cup/60 ml of the honey and refrigerate it, uncovered, overnight. (If the duck will not fit upright on the wine bottle in your refrigerator, remove the bottle and lay the duck, breast-side up, in the pan.)

4. Arrange a rack at center position and preheat the oven to 400°F/200°C/gas 6.

5. Bring the duck to room temperature for 30 minutes. Have ready a large, heavy roasting pan/tray and an adjustable roasting rack.

6. Season the duck cavity with ½ tsp salt and ½ tsp pepper, and then place three of the orange slices and the garlic cloves in the cavity. In a small bowl, whisk together the remaining ¼ cup/60 ml honey, 1 tbsp black pepper, orange zest, and orange juice. Brush half of this glaze over all surfaces of the duck. Place the duck, breast-side down, on the rack in the pan and roast for 20 minutes.

7. Reduce the temperature to 350°F/180°C/gas 4. Using tongs, turn the duck breast-side up on the rack and brush with half of the remaining glaze. If the wings or legs are starting to brown too quickly, cover them tightly with foil. Roast the duck for another 20 minutes and then brush with the remaining glaze. Continue to roast until a thermometer registers 170 to 180°F/77 to 82°C when inserted into the thickest part of the thigh, for 15 to 20 minutes more (see cooking tip). Watch carefully and cover any other areas of the duck that are browning too quickly with foil. Remove the duck to a carving board and tent loosely with foil. Let rest for 10 minutes.

8. While the duck is roasting, bring a large pot of salted water to a boil. Cook the potatoes until just tender when pierced with a knife, for about 10 minutes, then drain them and pat dry.

9. In a large frying pan, carefully pour ¼ cup/60 ml of the duck fat from the roasting pan; cool and refrigerate the remaining fat for another use. Place on medium-high heat; when the fat is hot, add the potatoes and cook, turning often, until golden brown, for about 10 minutes. Salt and pepper the potatoes.

10. To carve, using poultry shears or a sharp knife, cut the duck in half along each side of the breastbone. Cut each half in half again to separate the breast and wing quarter from the thigh and leg quarter. Arrange the quarters on a serving platter and surround them with potatoes. Garnish the platter with several bouquets of watercress and the remaining orange slices before serving.

SIDES: Brussels Sprouts, Bacon, and Apples (page 146) would make an excellent side for the duck and potatoes. You could also add a salad of baby spinach, Belgian endive, and walnuts tossed in a red wine vinaigrette to complete the menu.

LEFTOVER TIP: It's likely that you will have some duck fat left over after you prepare this dish. Do not throw it out. In France, duck fat is considered "liquid gold" and is used to add great flavor to sautéed foods.

COOKING TIP: The meat will be very pink at 170°F/77°C, and the juices will run a deep rosy pink. If you prefer the duck more well done, cook it to 180°F/82°C.

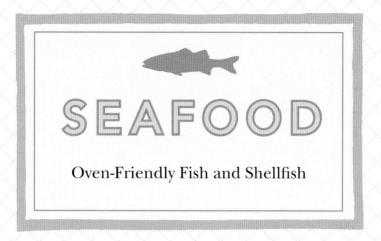

SEAFOOD

Oven-Friendly Fish and Shellfish

When it comes to fish, many cooks' first instinct is to panfry, deep-fry, boil, broil, or grill it. But there is another way: Roast it! Though this technique for preparing seafood may be less familiar to you, it is incredibly fast and easy and results in fish that is unfailingly moist.

Whether you want to roast whole or individual fillets or even shellfish, the guidelines are the same. Start out with the freshest and best catch possible. If you live in an inland area where it is not possible to buy fish straight from the ocean or stream, there are still good options. Look for fish that has been flash-frozen on the boat or dock just as soon as it is caught; it retains its flavor and texture nicely. Also, make a point of getting to know your local fish merchants. Ask when they receive deliveries and how the fish arrives in their store. Is it driven straight from the pier? Is it flown overnight from Asia? Once you've established a rapport, these vendors will be the first to point out specials and can also suggest alternatives when a fish you hope to purchase is not available.

In this section, you'll find recipes for roasting a variety of different fish and shellfish. For dinner with friends, you could serve a big, impressive whole fillet, like the Salmon Side with Fresh Orange-Ginger Relish or The Blue Heron's Striped Bass with Summer Herbs, Tomatoes, and Aioli. Both are gorgeous, fresh, and tasty.

Big, beefy cuts of tuna and swordfish, called steaks, take to oven cooking naturally. Sesame-Coated Tuna Steaks with Orange-Sherry Mayo and Swordfish Steaks with Fresh Corn Salsa are likely to please even your most die-hard meat eater. For seafood paired with bold seasonings, you won't go wrong with Roasted Cod with Tomatoes and Chunky Guacamole Salsa or with Halibut Steaks with Spinach, Chickpeas, and Bacon. Finally, shellfish is sublime when placed in a hot oven for only a few minutes, as you will discover with Skewered Shrimp with Warm Citrus Butter or Scallops Gratins with Lemon-Garlic Bread Crumbs.

Fast and fabulous—that's what I think of when it comes to roasting fish.

Roasted Cod with Tomatoes and Chunky Guacamole Salsa

When you've had a long day but still want to serve an attractive and delicious main course, this roasted cod is the answer. It's quick to assemble and needs only a short stay in a hot oven. Although cod is my favorite, other fish such as striped bass, grouper, or even halibut steaks also work well. The fish is drizzled with lime juice, and then topped with thinly sliced tomatoes. When roasted, the flesh is extra-moist and flakes easily. Garnishes include dollops of guacamole, a pinch of crumbled bacon, and a sprinkle of cilantro. The resulting dish, with its vibrant colors, looks as if it requires far more expertise and much more time than what is actually needed.

Serves 4

COST: Moderate

PREP TIME: 25 minutes, including making the guacamole

START-TO-FINISH TIME: 35 minutes

Olive oil for oiling the baking sheet/tray

2 cod fillets, 10 to 12 oz/280 to 340 g each and about ½ to ¾ in/12 mm to 2 cm thick

8 tsp fresh lime juice

Kosher salt

Freshly ground black pepper

2 to 3 medium tomatoes, stemmed and thinly sliced

4 slices bacon/streaky bacon (about 4 oz/ 115 g), fried until crisp and broken into bits

Chunky Guacamole Salsa (page 170; see market note)

4 tsp minced cilantro/fresh coriander

4 lime wedges, for garnish

SIDES: Blanched tender green beans and either buttered couscous or basmati rice scented with a hint of saffron would make easy and delicious sidekicks to the cod.

LEFTOVER TIP: Extra guacamole can be used as a dip with tortilla chips.

MARKET NOTE: Homemade guacamole is best, but if you are pressed for time, you can substitute a good-quality purchased one.

---

1. Arrange a rack at center position and preheat the oven to 425°F/220°C/gas 7.

2. Line a heavy, rimmed baking sheet/tray with foil and oil the foil generously. Arrange the fish fillets on the baking sheet/tray. Drizzle 4 tsp of lime juice over each fillet, then salt and pepper generously. Arrange slightly overlapping tomato slices on top of each fish to cover completely. (You may not need to use all of the tomatoes.)

3. Roast the fish until the flesh is opaque and flakes easily when pierced with a sharp knife, for 10 minutes or longer. (Cooking time will vary depending on the thickness of the fish so watch carefully.)

4. To serve, cut each fillet in half and, using a fish turner or a large metal spatula, transfer each piece to a dinner plate. Top each serving with a mound of the Chunky Guacamole Salsa, and sprinkle with some bacon and minced cilantro/ fresh coriander. Garnish with a lime wedge.

Halibut Steaks with Spinach, Chickpeas, and Bacon

On a visit to Barcelona, I ate a glorious lunch at Cal Pep, one of the Catalonian city's celebrated tapas bars. Among the endless parade of palate pleasers, an unusual sauté of spinach, chickpeas, and bacon caught my eye. At home I tried my own version of this delectable combo and topped it with roasted halibut steaks. The fish needs only about twelve minutes in the oven, just enough time for the spinach and chickpeas to be sautéed.

Serves 4

COST: Moderate to Splurge, depending on the season

PREP TIME: 15 minutes

START-TO-FINISH TIME: 30 minutes

4 tbsp/60 ml olive oil, plus more as needed

Two 1-lb/455-g halibut steaks, 1 in/2.5 cm thick

4 tbsp/60 ml fresh lemon juice

Kosher salt

Freshly ground black pepper

6 bacon slices (about 5 oz/140 g), cut into ½-in/12-mm pieces

One 15-oz/430-g can chickpeas, rinsed and drained well

10 oz/275 g baby spinach

2 tbsp minced flat-leaf parsley

Fleur de sel (optional)

Lemon wedges, for garnish

1. Arrange a rack at center position and preheat the oven to 450°F/230°C/gas 8.

2. Line a rimmed baking sheet/tray with foil and oil generously. Place the halibut steaks on the foil and drizzle each steak with 1 tbsp of lemon juice and 1 tbsp of oil. Salt and pepper the steaks.

3. Roast the fish until the flesh is opaque and flakes easily when pierced with a sharp knife, for about 12 minutes.

4. While the halibut is roasting, prepare the spinach and chickpeas. In a large, heavy frying pan over medium heat, fry the bacon pieces until golden and crisp, for about 3 minutes. Remove with a slotted spoon to drain on paper towels/absorbent paper. Discard the drippings in the frying pan and add the remaining 2 tbsp of oil. Heat until hot over medium heat.

5. Add the chickpeas to the frying pan and stir for 30 seconds. Add half of the spinach and stir until it starts to wilt, for about 1 minute. Add the rest of the spinach and stir constantly until all of the spinach has just wilted, for about 2 to 3 minutes; do not overcook. Remove from the heat and stir in the remaining 2 tbsp lemon juice and all but 2 tbsp of the bacon. Season with salt and pepper.

6. Spoon the spinach and chickpea mixture onto a serving platter and place the halibut steaks on top. Sprinkle the fish with parsley and with the remaining bacon. Season with fleur de sel, if desired. Garnish the platter with lemon wedges.

7. To serve, gently remove the skin by peeling it back from the flesh. Using a serving fork and spoon, lift the flesh away from the bones to get 2 servings from each steak. Accompany each serving with some of the sautéed chickpeas and spinach.

SIDES: Add a salad of mixed greens and tomatoes tossed in lemon juice and olive oil and a crusty loaf of peasant bread (sourdough is particularly good) to complete the offerings.

LEFTOVER TIP: If you have any remaining spinach-chickpea mixture, fill scooped-out tomato halves with it. Brush the tomatoes with olive oil and bake in a 350°F/180°C/gas 4 oven until tomatoes are tender and stuffing is warm, about 15 minutes.

Swordfish Steaks with Fresh Corn Salsa

Even fervent carnivores will be tempted by the delectable taste of these simple-to-prepare swordfish steaks. Thickly cut, the steaks are pan-seared, then roasted for a few minutes in the oven. A colorful corn salsa makes a vivid accompaniment to the succulent and tender fish.

Serves 4

COST: Moderate to Splurge, depending on the season

PREP TIME: 25 minutes, including making the salsa

START-TO-FINISH TIME: 35 minutes

Olive oil to coat the roasting pan/tray
Two 12-oz/340-g swordfish steaks, 1 in/2.5 cm thick
2 tbsp fresh lime juice
Kosher salt
Freshly ground black pepper
Fresh Corn Salsa (page 168)

1. Arrange a rack at center position and preheat the oven to 450°F/230°C/gas 8.

2. Place a large, heavy, ovenproof frying pan over high heat with enough oil to lightly coat the bottom. When the oil is very hot, add the swordfish steaks and sear on one side until just starting to brown, for about 2 minutes. Remove the pan from the heat and carefully turn the steaks. Pour 1 tbsp lime juice over each steak, and then salt and pepper them generously.

3. Place the pan in the oven and roast the fish until the flesh is opaque, for 6 to 8 minutes. Check for doneness by making a slit in the thickest part of a steak with a small, sharp knife.

4. Cut each steak in half and serve each portion mounded with some of the salsa.

SIDES: Roasted or blanched asparagus and buttered couscous sprinkled with minced chives would make easy accompaniments.

LEFTOVER TIP: Extra corn salsa can be used with other meats; it's especially good with pork, chicken, and turkey.

Sesame-Coated Tuna Steaks with Orange-Sherry Mayo

The only tuna I knew as a youngster came from a can, but later I discovered the fresh variety and became a devotee. Fresh tuna is endlessly versatile and cooks extremely quickly, especially when roasted. In the following recipe, tuna steaks, coated with sesame seeds, are pan-seared, then finished in the oven in less than five minutes. An orange-scented mayonnaise, prepared with good purchased mayo, takes minutes to assemble and makes a bracing garnish.

Serves 4

COST: Splurge

PREP TIME: 10 minutes, including making the mayo

START-TO-FINISH TIME: 20 minutes

COOKING TIP: Tuna can overcook easily and turn dry, so it needs only a very short time in the oven. It is best when cooked to medium-rare, which means that there should be a thin line of slightly uncooked meat than runs through the center of each steak.

Mayo

½ cup/120 ml good-quality mayonnaise

1 tbsp minced flat-leaf parsley

2 tsp finely chopped shallots

1½ tsp dry sherry

1¼ tsp grated orange zest

Tuna

1 egg white, beaten lightly

½ cup/70 g sesame seeds

Kosher salt

Freshly ground black pepper

4 tuna steaks, each 5½ to 6 oz/155 to 170 g and about 1 in/2.5 cm thick

Canola oil to coat the frying pan

1 tbsp minced flat-leaf parsley, for garnish

SIDES: Blanched snow peas and white rice tossed with chopped scallions, minced ginger, and a hint of sesame oil would make easy and tempting sides.

LEFTOVER TIP: Although this tuna is best eaten immediately, any extra can be flaked and added to a watercress and green onion salad tossed in orange juice, white wine vinegar, and olive oil.

FOR THE MAYO:

Whisk together the mayonnaise, parsley, shallots, sherry, and orange zest in a medium bowl. (The mayo can be prepared 4 hours ahead; cover and refrigerate. Bring to room temperature 30 minutes before using.)

FOR THE TUNA:

1. Arrange a rack at center position and preheat the oven to 450°F/230°C/gas 8.

2. Place the egg white in a small bowl and spread the sesame seeds on a dinner plate. Salt and pepper the tuna on both sides. Brush each steak with some egg white, then coat both sides with sesame seeds.

3. Use enough canola oil to lightly cover the bottom of a large, heavy, ovenproof frying pan. Place the pan over medium heat and, when the oil is hot, sear the steaks for 1 minute, then turn and sear the other side for only 30 seconds. Place the frying pan in the oven and roast for 2 minutes, then, using a metal spatula, turn the steaks and roast for another 2 minutes for medium-rare (see cooking tip).

4. Remove the pan from the oven and transfer the steaks to 4 dinner plates. Garnish each serving with a dollop of the mayo and a sprinkle of parsley.

Skewers of Peppered Tuna with Wasabi Mayo

On my sole visit to Japan, I was determined to visit Tsukiji, the celebrated fish market in the center of Tokyo. I rose very early in the morning and walked in the dark, accompanied by my half-asleep husband, from our hotel to the market. As we arrived, just in time, I heard the bell ring for the tuna auction. I was stunned by the size of the tuna on display: They were enormous, weighing in at hundreds of pounds. The amount of tuna called for in this dish is a mere fraction of those huge fish, but the recipe's Japanese accents bring back memories of that remarkable visit. Cubes of tuna are marinated in soy, and then skewered with pickled ginger before being quickly roasted. A bowl of peppery wasabi-scented mayonnaise accompanies the fish.

Serves 4

COST: Splurge

PREP TIME: 10 minutes

START-TO-FINISH TIME: 1 hour

MATERIALS: Four 10-in/ 25-cm (or longer) metal skewers, or wooden skewers that have been soaked in water for 30 minutes

Wasabi Mayo

2 tbsp wasabi powder (available at many supermarkets in the Asian food section)

½ cup/120 ml good-quality mayonnaise

Tuna

1¼ lb/570 g fresh boneless tuna

2½ tbsp soy sauce

2 tsp coarsely ground black pepper

1 small jar pickled ginger

Canola oil for greasing the baking sheet/tray

A bunch of watercress

FOR THE WASABI MAYO:

Use a fork to mix together the wasabi powder and 1 tbsp water in a small bowl. Stir in the mayonnaise. (The Wasabi Mayo can be prepared 1 day ahead; cover and refrigerate. Bring to room temperature 30 minutes before using.)

FOR THE TUNA:

1. Cut the tuna into 1-in/2.5-cm cubes, and then place them in a shallow dish and toss with the soy sauce. Marinate at cool room temperature for 30 to 45 minutes, turning once or twice. Remove the cubes and pat dry. Place the tuna in another bowl and toss with the pepper to coat well.

2. Cut the pickled ginger into 20 to 24 ribbons that are 2 to 3 in/5 to 7.5 cm long.

3. Arrange a rack at center position and preheat the oven to 450°F/230°C/gas 8. Line a baking sheet/tray with foil and oil it generously.

4. Skewer the tuna cubes alternately with the pickled ginger. You should get six or more cubes per skewer. Arrange the skewers on the baking sheet/tray and roast for about 4 minutes for medium-rare in the center (see cooking tip, page 123).

5. Serve each skewer on a dinner plate on a bed of watercress. Pass a bowl of Wasabi Mayo.

SIDES: 5-Minute Roasted Sugar Snap Peas (page 149) and white rice tossed with minced chives, toasted sesame seeds, and a little sesame oil would make fine sides.

LEFTOVER TIP: This tuna is best cooked and eaten immediately, but any remaining cubes are good served cold and topped with dollops of wasabi mayo as an appetizer.

Salmon Fillets on a Bed of Peas

Coral-hued salmon resting upon a verdant field of spring peas is a tempting sight. This visually impressive dish looks sophisticated, but is actually quite easy to assemble. Both the salmon and the peas are seasoned with a flavorful mixture of parsley, butter, shallots, and lemon that are whizzed together in a food processor. The fillets need less than fifteen minutes of roasting time, and while they are in the oven, the peas can be quickly blanched.

Serves 4

COST: Moderate

PREP TIME: 15 minutes

START-TO-FINISH TIME: 40 minutes, including roasting the salmon

5 tbsp/70 g unsalted butter,
   at room temperature
2 tbsp minced flat-leaf parsley
2 tbsp chopped shallots
1 tsp minced garlic
1 tsp grated lemon zest, plus thin lemon slices
   for garnish (optional)
Kosher salt
Olive oil for greasing the baking sheet/tray
4 salmon fillets, about 6 oz/170 g each
   and ¾ in/2 cm thick
6 tsp fresh lemon juice
Freshly ground black pepper
3 cups/455 g fresh peas or a 16-oz/
   455-g bag frozen peas, defrosted
Parsley or watercress sprigs for garnish

1. Combine the butter, parsley, shallots, garlic, lemon zest, and ¼ tsp salt in a food processor; pulse to combine, for about 30 seconds. (The butter mixture can be prepared 1 day ahead; cover and refrigerate. Bring to room temperature before using.)

2. Arrange a rack at center position and preheat the oven to 450°F/230°C/gas 8. Line a rimmed baking sheet/tray with foil and oil well.

3. Place the salmon fillets, skin-side down, on the baking sheet/tray, and sprinkle each one with 1½ tsp lemon juice and season generously with salt and pepper. Let rest for 10 minutes.

4. Reserve 3 tbsp of the butter mixture for seasoning the peas. With a metal spatula or table knife, spread the remaining butter evenly over the tops of the fillets. Roast the salmon until the flesh flakes easily when pierced with a knife and is opaque, for about 12 minutes, depending on the thickness of the fish.

continued...

5. While the salmon is roasting, bring a medium pot of water to a boil. Add 1 tsp salt and the peas and cook until the peas are just tender, for 3 to 4 minutes for fresh and for 2 minutes for frozen. Drain the peas and return them to the pot. Toss them with the reserved 3 tbsp butter and season with salt.

6. To serve, spread the peas on a platter and arrange the salmon on top. Garnish each fillet with a parsley or watercress sprig and, if desired, with a lemon slice.

SIDES: Serve baby red potatoes sprinkled with sea salt or basmati rice scented lightly with saffron. To complete the menu, add a salad of mixed greens, thinly sliced cucumbers, and sweet red onion tossed in a vinaigrette.

LEFTOVER TIP: Flake any remaining salmon and combine with leftover peas, some chopped green/spring onions, and goat cheese; use as the filling for an omelet.

Salmon Side with Fresh Orange-Ginger Relish

This is an unusual and impressive way to serve salmon. Instead of using individual-sized portions, a salmon fillet is roasted whole, and then garnished with a fresh orange and ginger relish. Because the salmon is marinated for several hours before it goes into the oven, the fish is moist and well seasoned when done.

Serves 6 to 8

COST: Moderate

PREP TIME: 35 minutes, including making the Orange-Ginger Relish

START-TO-FINISH TIME: 3 to 5 hours depending on how long the fish is marinated

⅓ cup/75 ml dry white wine

⅓ cup/75 ml fresh orange juice

2½ tbsp soy sauce

One 2½-lb/1.2-kg salmon fillet half, about 1 in/2.5 cm thick in the center section

Vegetable oil for greasing the baking sheet/tray

Kosher salt

Freshly ground black pepper

Orange-Ginger Relish (page 166)

SIDES: Buttered basmati rice sprinkled with minced chives and 5-Minute Roasted Sugar Snap Peas (page 149) would make ideal sides to this main course. Or serve the salmon with roasted asparagus and buttered couscous.

LEFTOVER TIP: Flake any remaining salmon and add to a watercress and cucumber salad tossed in a white wine vinaigrette.

1. In a small bowl, whisk together the wine, orange juice, and soy sauce and pour into a 9-by-13-by-2-in/33-cm-by-23-cm-by-5 cm baking dish. Carefully lay the salmon, skin-side up, in the dish. Cover with plastic wrap/cling film and refrigerate for at least 2 hours or up to 4 hours. Bring to room temperature for 30 minutes before roasting.

2. Arrange a rack at center position and preheat the oven to 450°F/230°C/gas 8.

3. Line a heavy, rimmed baking sheet/tray with foil and brush generously with oil. Remove the fish from the marinade and pat dry with paper towels/absorbent paper. Brush the salmon skin with oil and arrange skin-side down on the baking sheet/tray. (If the salmon is longer than your baking sheet/tray, arrange it on the diagonal.) Salt and pepper the fillet.

4. Roast the salmon until the flesh is opaque in the center, for about 20 minutes. Remove the baking sheet/tray from the oven, and use a large metal spatula to loosen the salmon from the foil. Using the foil as an aid and wearing oven mitts, carefully lift the salmon from the baking sheet/tray and let it slide from the foil onto a serving platter.

5. To serve, mound some Orange-Ginger Relish down the center along the length of the salmon and pass the remaining relish alongside.

The Blue Heron's Striped Bass with Summer Herbs, Tomatoes, and Aioli

The creation of gifted chef Deborah Snow of the Blue Heron Restaurant in Sunderland, Massachusetts, this is a glorious dish to serve when summer herbs and tomatoes are in season. Striped bass is roasted simply with lemon juice and olive oil, then dressed up with a multihued cherry tomato salad. A bowl of easy-to-make aioli complements this fish beautifully. You can serve the fish straight from the oven or offer it at room temperature, with equally tempting results.

Serves 6

COST: Moderate to Splurge, depending on the season

PREP TIME: 35 minutes

START-TO-FINISH TIME: 1 hour

Tomato Salad

2 cups/345 g cherry or grape tomatoes (see market note, page 132)

½ cup/65 g chopped or thinly sliced red onion

1 tsp minced garlic

3 tbsp olive oil

1 tbsp fresh lemon juice

½ tsp kosher salt

Freshly ground black pepper

1 tbsp minced or 2 tbsp torn fresh basil

1 tbsp minced or 2 tbsp torn fresh flat-leaf parsley

1 tbsp minced or 2 tbsp torn fresh mint

2 tsp minced or 1½ tbsp torn cilantro/fresh coriander

Striped Bass

1½ tbsp olive oil, plus more for greasing the baking sheet/tray and the fish

1 boneless striped bass fillet, 2 to 2½ lb/ 910 g to 1.2 kg (see market note)

Kosher salt

Freshly ground black pepper

1½ tbsp fresh lemon juice

1 tbsp dry white wine

Aioli (page 174)

FOR THE TOMATO SALAD:

Combine the tomatoes, onion, and garlic in a large mixing bowl. In a small bowl, whisk together the olive oil, lemon juice, salt, and several grinds of pepper. Pour over the tomatoes and mix. (The salad can be prepared to this point 2 hours ahead; leave uncovered at room temperature. The herbs are added right before serving.)

continued...

FOR THE STRIPED BASS:

1. Arrange a rack at center position and preheat the oven to 400°F/200°C/gas 6.

2. Line a rimmed baking sheet/tray with foil and oil it generously. Brush the skin side of the fillet with oil and place the fish, skin-side down, on the baking sheet/tray. Season the fish with salt and pepper, then drizzle with the lemon juice and wine, and finally with the 1½ tbsp olive oil. Roast the fish until the flesh is opaque and flakes easily, for about 20 minutes.

3. While the fish is in the oven, stir the basil, parsley, mint, and cilantro into the tomato salad and toss to mix well.

4. Using two metal spatulas, carefully transfer the striped bass to a large platter. Spoon the tomato salad on top. Serve warm or at room temperature with a bowl of aioli.

SIDES: Tender green beans seasoned with sea salt, and a crusty baguette or peasant loaf would complete this menu.

LEFTOVER TIP: Extra fish is good served at room temperature with a dollop of aioli for a light lunch.

MARKET NOTES: You can use any small colorful tomatoes, preferably not more than about 2 in/ 5 cm in diameter. I typically buy red, yellow, and orange cherry tomatoes and add some small green, orange, or red heirlooms. You can leave the tomatoes whole or halve them.

If you can't find striped bass, you can substitute halibut steaks or swordfish.

Skewered Shrimp with Warm Citrus Butter

You might think that the only way to cook skewered shrimp is to throw them on the grill or pop them under the broiler, but there is another alternative. As it turns out, roasting shrimp is incredibly easy and practically fail-proof. In the following recipe, extra-large shrimp are threaded on skewers, brushed with melted butter that is scented with orange and lemon, and then placed in the oven for only a few minutes. There's no need to turn the shrimp as they roast to a rich rosy hue. For eating, the shrimp are dipped in more of the warm citrus butter.

Serves 4

COST: Moderate

PREP TIME: 15 minutes

START-TO-FINISH TIME: 25 minutes

MATERIALS: Four 10-in/25-cm metal skewers, or wooden skewers that have been soaked in water for 30 minutes

---

6 tbsp/85 g unsalted butter, cut into small chunks

1 tsp grated orange zest, plus ⅓ cup/75 ml fresh orange juice

1 tbsp fresh lemon juice

2 tsp toasted sesame oil

20 extra-large (16 to 20 count) shrimp/prawns, about 1 to 1¼ lb/455 to 570 g, peeled and deveined with tails left on

Kosher salt

Freshly ground black pepper

2 tsp sesame seeds, toasted (see cooking tip)

SIDES: Serve with Skillet Summer Corn (page 154) and with tender green beans sprinkled with sea salt.

LEFTOVER TIP: If you have any shrimp/prawns left over (highly unlikely!), add them to a green salad tossed in lemon juice and olive oil.

COOKING TIP: To toast sesame seeds, place them in a medium frying pan set over medium heat. Stir until the seeds are golden brown, for 3 to 5 minutes. Remove and cool. Sesame seeds can be toasted 2 hours ahead. Leave at room temperature.

---

1. Place the butter, orange zest, orange juice, lemon juice, and sesame oil in a small nonreactive saucepan. Set over medium heat and stir until the butter has melted and the mixture is just warm. (The citrus butter can be prepared 2 hours ahead; cover and leave at room temperature. Reheat when ready to use.)

2. Arrange a rack at center position and preheat the oven to 450°F/230°C/gas 8.

3. Place 5 shrimp/prawns on each skewer and arrange the skewers on a baking sheet/tray. Remove ¼ cup/60 ml of the citrus butter and use it to brush the shrimp/prawns on both sides. Reserve the remaining butter to use as a dipping sauce. Salt and pepper the shrimp/prawns.

4. Roast the shrimp/prawns until they are opaque, pink, and cooked all the way through, for 5 to 6 minutes. Remove from the oven and sprinkle the shrimp/prawns with sesame seeds. Divide the remaining butter among four small ramekins, and serve with the skewers.

Scallop Gratins with Lemon-Garlic Bread Crumbs

My son, a talented amateur cook, often calls to tell me about new recipes. During one such conversation, he couldn't wait to describe these scallop gratins, which need only minutes to cook, and when done, are irresistible with crisp, golden crusts covering succulent morsels of seafood. I've made this dish countless times. I keep the recipe in a file labeled "fresh, fast, and fabulous!"

Serves 4

COST: Moderate

PREP TIME: 25 minutes, including making the fresh bread crumbs

START-TO-FINISH TIME: 40 minutes

4 tbsp/8 g minced flat-leaf parsley

4 tbsp/55 g unsalted butter, at room temperature

1 tbsp finely chopped shallots

4 tsp minced garlic (about 2 medium cloves)

1½ tsp grated lemon zest

Kosher salt

1½ tbsp olive oil

1½ cups/85 g fresh coarse bread crumbs made from a baguette or peasant loaf (see cooking tip, page 49)

1½ lb/680 g fresh sea scallops, side muscles removed

Freshly ground black pepper

NOTE: I have also used 1-cup/240-ml ramekins in place of gratin or crème brûlée dishes. They work well and the cooking time is the same, but the gratin dishes make a nicer presentation.

SIDES: Serve these gratins with corn on the cob along with a salad of watercress and cucumber tossed in a vinaigrette.

LEFTOVER TIP: If you should have any scallops left over, slice them into thin rounds and use them as a garnish for a creamy vegetable soup whose flavors are complementary to this shellfish, such as cream of asparagus, watercress, or carrot soup. The heat of the soup will warm the thinly sliced scallops.

1. Combine the parsley, 3 tbsp of the butter, shallots, garlic, lemon zest, and ½ tsp salt in a small nonreactive mixing bowl. Mix well with a fork or spoon to blend. (The butter can be made 1 day ahead. Cover tightly and refrigerate. Bring to room temperature before using.)

2. Heat the oil in a medium, heavy frying pan over medium heat. When hot, add the bread crumbs and cook, stirring constantly, until they are crisp and a rich golden brown, for 3 to 4 minutes. Transfer the bread crumbs to a dinner plate. (The bread crumbs can be prepared 3 hours ahead. Cover with plastic wrap/cling film and leave at room temperature.)

3. Arrange a rack at center position and preheat the oven to 400°F/200°C/gas 6.

4. Using some of the seasoned butter, grease the bottom and sides of four 4-in/10-cm round individual gratin or crème brûlée dishes. Divide the scallops evenly among the dishes, placing them so they fit tightly in a single layer in each dish. Pat one-fourth of the seasoned butter on top of each portion, pushing some of the butter down into the crevices between the scallops. Salt and pepper the scallops well. Divide the bread crumbs evenly and spread on top of the scallops in each dish. Cut the remaining 1 tbsp of unseasoned butter into cubes and dot each portion with them.

5. Place the dishes on a baking sheet/tray and roast until the scallops are cooked through, for about 12 minutes. To check for doneness, gently pierce the bread-crumb layer with a small knife to see if the shellfish beneath are opaque.

6. Serve immediately.

SIDES

Simple yet Satisfying Partners

You've decided on the roast, you've checked in with the butcher or the fishmonger, but you still haven't chosen the sides. Chances are you haven't paid much attention to them. Ideally, side dishes should play supporting roles, complementing and enhancing the star attraction. In a pinch, plain buttered potatoes and a salad will certainly do, but with just a little extra effort you can produce even more tantalizing possibilities.

You don't have to give up on potatoes. Just dress them up a little. Beef and pork roasts, in particular, partner beautifully with Golden Potato Gratin or with Best-Ever Mashed Potatoes and Five Variations. Both of these dishes can be prepared completely in advance. Yorkshire Pudding with Bacon and Sage is my favorite pairing with a standing rib roast. The two dishes are elegant, traditional, and hearty—all at once! For roast turkey and other fowl, Sourdough Dressing with Roasted Root Vegetables or Wild Rice with Roasted Grapes and Walnuts make delectable embellishments.

You'll find a number of seasonal vegetable creations for both warm and cold weather on the following pages. Unique 5-Minute Roasted Sugar Snap Peas, fabulous Skillet Summer Corn, and colorful Zucchini and Tomato Gratin are bright and refreshing sides for spring and summer. In the fall and winter, try Honey-Glazed Carrots and Parsnips or Brussels Sprouts, Bacon, and Apples.

Far from being afterthoughts, side dishes should accentuate your roasts, highlighting their textures and flavors. There are more than a dozen recipes for inventive sides in this chapter—enough to give you plenty of choices, whatever you roast.

Best-Ever Mashed Potatoes and Five Variations

Nothing is a better match for a roast than mashed potatoes. Creamy, buttered spuds are the hands-down favorite side dish whether it's roasted red meat, poultry, or fish. The classic mashed potatoes featured here are enriched by an unexpected but delicious addition of tender, sautéed leeks. Besides this basic recipe, there are five easy variations—enough to provide you with plenty of choices whenever a roast is on your menu.

Serves 4 to 6

COST: Inexpensive

PREP TIME: 10 minutes

START-TO-FINISH TIME: 30 to 35 minutes

2 lb/910 g Yukon gold potatoes, peeled and cut into 1-in/2.5-cm dice

Kosher salt

2 tbsp unsalted butter

2 cups/160 g finely chopped leeks, white and light green parts only (3 to 4 leeks)

½ cup/120 ml reduced-sodium chicken broth

½ cup/120 ml whole milk, plus more if needed

Freshly ground black pepper

1½ tbsp minced flat-leaf parsley

1. Bring a large pot of water to a boil. Add the potatoes and 1 tbsp salt. Cook until the potatoes are tender, for about 15 minutes.

2. Meanwhile, prepare the leeks. Heat the butter in a medium, heavy frying pan over medium-low heat. When hot, add the leeks and cook, stirring, until softened but not browned, for 4 to 5 minutes. Watch carefully and lower the heat if necessary. Add the broth and cook until almost all liquids have evaporated, for about 4 to 5 minutes or longer.

3. When done, drain the potatoes and return them to their pot. Mash with a potato masher, then stir in the milk and leeks. Season with salt and pepper. Add more milk for creamier potatoes. Cover the potatoes to keep them warm for up to 20 minutes. (The potatoes can be prepared 4 hours ahead; cover and refrigerate. Reheat over low heat, stirring constantly and adding a little extra milk if needed, until warm, or reheat them in a bowl in the microwave.) Mound the potatoes in a bowl and sprinkle them with parsley.

SERVE WITH: These potatoes could accompany most of the roasts in this book, other than those dishes in which potatoes are cooked along with the roasts.

The variations pair well with specific main courses. For example, the Fennel and Tarragon version partners successfully with salmon and lamb, while the Blue Cheese variation is particularly good with beef. The Creamy Goat Cheese and Thyme and the Provencal Basil adaptations are excellent with many lamb and fish recipes. Finally, the Buttermilk-Country Mustard variation makes a fine side to roast pork and chicken.

Fennel and Tarragon

Add 2 tsp crushed fennel seeds and replace the parsley with 1½ tbsp fresh minced tarragon.

Blue Cheese

Stir in ⅓ lb/155 g crumbled creamy blue cheese (at room temperature), such as Bleu d'Auvergne, when you add the leeks. For a stronger blue cheese taste, add more cheese.

Provencal Basil

Place the milk and ½ cup/25 g packed fresh torn basil leaves in a small saucepan set over medium heat. Stir until the leaves have wilted and the milk is warm, for only 1 to 2 minutes. Puree this mixture in a food processor until the basil is minced, then stir into the potatoes. Omit the parsley in the original recipe.

Buttermilk–Country Mustard

Replace the milk with buttermilk and stir in 1 tbsp whole-grain Dijon mustard.

Creamy Goat Cheese and Thyme

Stir in 7 oz/200 g creamy goat cheese (at room temperature) when you add the leeks. Replace the parsley with 1½ tsp fresh minced thyme.

Golden Potato Gratin

For this scrumptious gratin, three layers of sliced Yukon golds, each coated with crème fraîche and heavy cream and seasoned with a hint of thyme, are baked until crisp and golden on top and fork-tender beneath. This dish can be made completely in advance, and then reheated quickly at serving time.

Serves 8

COST: Moderate

PREP TIME: 15 minutes

START-TO-FINISH TIME: 1 hour, 30 minutes, including resting time for the gratin

1 tbsp unsalted butter for greasing the baking dish
1½ cups/360 ml crème fraîche
⅓ cup/75 ml heavy/double cream
3 lb/1.4 kg Yukon gold potatoes, peeled and cut into ⅛-in-/3-mm-thick rounds
Kosher salt
Freshly ground black pepper
1½ tsp dried thyme leaves

SERVE WITH: This gratin makes a tempting side to many of the beef roasts in Chapter 1, especially Beef Tenderloin with Roasted Shallots, Bacon, and Port (page 32) and Beef Tenderloin Stuffed with Spinach, Mascarpone, and Sun-Dried Tomatoes (page 35). It also complements Ham with an Orange Marmalade Glaze and Rhubarb Chutney (page 63) and Roast Veal with Tarragon-Mustard Butter (page 81).

1. Arrange a rack at center position and preheat the oven to 400°F/200°C/gas 6.

2. Butter a 3½- to 4-quart/3.3- to 3.8-L oven-to-table baking dish generously (a 9-by-13-in/23-by-33-cm dish works well).

3. In a medium bowl, whisk together the crème fraîche and the cream.

4. Arrange one-third of the potato slices in the bottom of the prepared pan, overlapping them slightly. Season them generously with salt and pepper and with ½ tsp of the thyme. Spread one-third of the crème fraîche mixture over the potatoes. Repeat to make two more layers.

5. Bake for 30 minutes, then reduce the heat to 350°F/180°C/gas 4 and cook until the potatoes are tender when pierced with a sharp knife and the top is golden brown, for about 25 minutes more. Let rest for 20 minutes before serving. (The gratin can be prepared 4 hours ahead; cool, cover loosely with foil, and leave at cool room temperature. Reheat, uncovered, in a preheated 350°F/180°C/gas 4 oven until hot, for about 15 minutes.)

Zucchini and Tomato Gratin

This gratin is composed of two layers of sautéed zucchini slices with a single layer of sliced tomatoes tucked in between. The vegetables are topped with a fresh bread crumb and Parmesan mixture, and then dotted with bits of feta cheese. When baked, the zucchini and tomatoes soften and meld into each other, while the crust becomes golden and crisp. For those who love to cook in advance, this dish is a dream. It can be assembled and baked several hours ahead, then reheated when needed.

Serves 4 to 6

COST: Inexpensive

PREP TIME: 20 minutes, including making the fresh bread crumbs

START-TO-FINISH TIME: 1 hour, 15 minutes, including time for the gratin to rest

About ½ cup/120 ml olive oil

2 lb/910 g (about 6 medium) zucchini/courgette

1 lb/455 g tomatoes

Kosher salt

Freshly ground black pepper

1½ tsp dried crushed rosemary (see cooking tip, page 19)

6 tbsp/23 g fresh bread crumbs, preferably made from a baguette or peasant bread without crusts (see cooking tip, page 49)

6 tbsp/45 g grated Parmigiano-Reggiano cheese

⅓ cup/55 g crumbled feta

2 tbsp pine nuts (optional)

Fresh rosemary sprigs, for garnish (optional)

1. Arrange a rack at center position and preheat the oven to 425°F/220°C/gas 7. Oil a large (2 quart/2 L) baking dish with some of the olive oil.

2. Trim and discard the ends from the zucchini/courgette and cut them into slices ¼ in/6 mm thick. Stem the tomatoes and cut them into slices ¼ in/6 mm thick.

3. Set one extra-large frying pan over medium heat and add about 2 tbsp oil or enough to coat the bottom of the pan. When hot, add enough zucchini/courgette slices to the pan to fit snugly in a single layer. Cook, turning several times, until the slices are well browned on both sides and very tender when pierced with a knife, for about 8 minutes. Remove and drain on paper towels/absorbent paper. Repeat with the remaining zucchini/courgette, adding more oil to the pan as needed.

4. Arrange half of the zucchini/courgette slices, slightly overlapping, in the baking dish; salt and pepper them, then sprinkle with ½ tsp of the rosemary. Arrange the tomato slices, slightly overlapping, over the zucchini/courgette. Salt and pepper them, then sprinkle with ½ tsp rosemary. Make a final layer with the remaining zucchini/courgette. Salt and pepper them and sprinkle with the remaining rosemary.

5. For the topping, combine the bread crumbs and Parmigiano cheese in a bowl and spread over the vegetables. Dot with feta, and, if you like, sprinkle with pine nuts. Drizzle the gratin with 1 tbsp of olive oil. Bake until the vegetables are tender and the topping is golden and crisp, for about 20 minutes. (The gratin can be prepared 3 hours ahead; cool, then cover loosely with foil and leave at cool room temperature. Reheat in a preheated 350°F/180°C/gas 4 oven for about 15 minutes. Cover the top loosely with foil if it starts to brown too much.)

6. Cool the gratin for 10 minutes before serving. Garnish the gratin with some fresh rosemary sprigs, if desired.

SERVE WITH: This gratin makes a fine garnish to roast lamb, veal, chicken, or fish. Try it with Roast Veal with Tarragon-Mustard Butter (page 81) or Chicken Quarters Roasted with Lemons and Green Olives (page 97).

Butternut Squash with Walnut–Goat Cheese Crumble

Although this dish calls for only a few ingredients, it delivers big, robust flavors and can be prepared almost completely in advance. The diced squash can be roasted several hours ahead so that at serving time all that is necessary is to arrange the cubes on a platter and sprinkle them with crumbled goat cheese, chopped walnuts, and minced parsley. My local supermarkets sell butternut squash that is already peeled and halved, and if you can find it in this convenient form, it will shave a good amount of time off the prep.

Serves 6

COST: Moderate

PREP TIME: 20 minutes if you purchase peeled butternut squash; 40 minutes if you peel and cube it yourself

START-TO-FINISH TIME: 55 minutes to 1¼ hours

3 tbsp olive oil

3 lb/1.4 kg butternut squash, peeled and cut into 1-in/2.5-cm dice to make 8 cups (see market note)

Kosher salt

Freshly ground black pepper

½ cup/55 g walnuts, toasted and coarsely chopped (see cooking tip)

½ cup/115 g goat cheese, crumbled

2 tbsp minced flat-leaf parsley

MARKET NOTE: Look for peeled butternut squash in the produce section of the supermarket. About 40 oz/1.2 kg of this peeled squash should yield 8 cups. If you buy a whole squash, look for one that weighs 2½ to 3 lb/1.2 to 1.4 kg, before peeling.

COOKING TIP: To toast the walnuts, spread them on a rimmed baking sheet/tray and place in a preheated 350°F/180°C/gas 4 oven until lightly browned and fragrant, 5 to 6 minutes. Watch carefully so that they do not burn. Remove and cool.

1. Arrange a rack at center position and preheat the oven to 375°F/190°C/gas 5.

2. Brush a heavy, rimmed baking sheet/tray with 1 tbsp of the oil. Spread the cubed squash in a single layer on the baking sheet/tray. Drizzle the remaining 2 tbsp oil over the squash, and toss to coat well. Season with 1 tsp salt and several grinds of black pepper.

3. Roast the squash, stirring every 10 minutes, until it is tender when pierced with a knife and browned around the edges, for about 35 minutes or longer. Remove and set aside. (The squash can be roasted 1 day ahead. Cool, cover, and refrigerate. When ready to serve, reheat in a 350°F/180°C/gas 4 oven until warm, for about 15 minutes.)

4. Place the roasted squash cubes on a serving platter and sprinkle with walnuts, goat cheese, and parsley.

SERVE WITH: This dish is particularly good with roast poultry. Try it with Golden Cider-Roasted Turkey (page 99), "Never Fail" Roast Turkey with Shallot Pan Gravy (page 102), or with Cornish Hens with Orange-Cherry Sauce (page 112).

Honey-Glazed Carrots and Parsnips

I was stunned at Thanksgiving several years ago when I saw family members filling their plates not only with seconds of turkey and dressing, but also with mounds of roasted carrots and parsnips—a humble combination of vegetables if ever there were one. This side dish could not be easier to prepare. The root vegetables need only a half hour in the oven to become charred on the outside and silky smooth inside. They're finished with a glaze made with honey, butter, and balsamic vinegar.

Serves 8

COST: Inexpensive

PREP TIME: 20 minutes

START-TO-FINISH TIME: 55 minutes

2 lb/910 g slim carrots, peeled and halved lengthwise

2 lb/910 g slim parsnips, peeled and halved lengthwise

6 tbsp/90 ml olive oil, plus 1 to 2 tbsp more as needed

Kosher salt

Freshly ground black pepper

1½ tbsp unsalted butter

1½ tbsp honey

1 tsp balsamic vinegar

SERVE WITH: This colorful dish makes a great side for Golden Cider-Roasted Turkey (page 99), "Never Fail" Roast Turkey with Shallot Pan Gravy (page 102), and Cornish Hens with Fennel and Fingerlings (page 109).

1. Arrange one rack at center position and another at a lower position and preheat the oven to 400°F/200°C/gas 6. Line two large, rimmed baking sheets/trays with foil.

2. Divide the carrots and parsnips evenly between the pans. Drizzle the vegetables in each pan with 3 tbsp olive oil, and then stir with a wooden spoon until vegetables are coated. Add 1 to 2 tbsp more oil if needed. Season the vegetables with 1 tsp of salt and several grinds of pepper.

3. Roast the vegetables, stirring with a wooden spoon every 10 minutes, until slightly charred on the outside and tender when pierced with a knife, for 30 to 35 minutes. After 20 minutes, reverse the pans top to bottom. When done, remove and cover the vegetables loosely with foil to keep them warm. (The vegetables can be prepared 4 hours ahead; cool to room temperature and cover loosely with foil. Reheat uncovered in a 350°F/180°C/gas 4 oven for about 10 minutes.)

4. In a small saucepan set over medium heat, melt the butter, then remove the pan from the heat, and stir in the honey and vinegar. (The sauce can be prepared 4 hours ahead; leave at cool room temperature; reheat over medium heat, stirring constantly.)

5. Transfer the carrots and parsnips to a serving platter. Taste and season with more salt and pepper if needed. Drizzle the honey mixture over the vegetables and toss gently.

Brussels Sprouts, Bacon, and Apples

Three unlikely cohorts–assertive Brussels sprouts, salty bacon, and sweet apples–combine to make this winning side dish. The humble sprouts acquire a surprising and delicious flavor when paired with the sautéed apples and bacon. Even the pickiest eaters will find this cold-weather vegetable tempting prepared this way.

Serves 4

COST: Inexpensive

PREP TIME: 10 minutes

START-TO-FINISH TIME: 35 minutes

1 lb/455 g Brussels sprouts

Kosher salt

4 or 5 thick bacon slices (about 4 oz/115 g), cut crosswise into ½-in/12-mm pieces

1½ tbsp unsalted butter

2 large Golden Delicious apples, peeled, halved, cored, and cut into 1-in/2.5-cm cubes

1½ tbsp minced flat-leaf parsley (optional)

SERVE WITH: This vegetable combo is good with roasted turkey, chicken, and pork. Try it with "Never Fail" Roast Turkey with Shallot Pan Gravy (page 102) or Crown Roast of Pork with Tarragon-Mustard Butter (page 52).

1. Cut off and discard the bases from the Brussels sprouts, then halve the sprouts. Bring a large pot of water to a boil and add the sprouts and 2 tsp salt. Cook until the sprouts are tender but not mushy when pierced with a small, sharp knife, for 8 to 10 minutes or longer. (Cooking time can vary depending on the size of the Brussels sprouts.)

2. Drain the sprouts in a colander, then place them (still in the colander) under cold running water until completely cool. Pat them dry and set aside. (Brussels sprouts can be prepared 6 hours ahead; cover and refrigerate. Bring to room temperature before using.)

3. Sauté the bacon in a large, heavy frying pan over medium heat until browned and crisp. Remove it with a slotted spoon to drain on paper towels/absorbent paper. Pour off and discard all but 2 tsp of the drippings in the pan. Return the pan to medium heat and add the butter. When hot, add the apples and cook, turning often, until softened and just lightly browned, for about 5 minutes. Add the Brussels sprouts and bacon to the frying pan. Stir and cook until all ingredients are heated through, for 2 to 3 minutes. Season with salt.

4. Mound the vegetables in a serving bowl and, if desired, sprinkle with parsley. Serve hot.

Sautéed Spinach with Blue Cheese and Hazelnuts

Blue cheese adds a distinctive flavoring to this dish of sautéed fresh spinach. Half of the cheese is stirred right into the frying pan and melts to form a delectable sauce for the greens. The remainder is crumbled and used along with chopped hazelnuts as a garnish. Goat cheese can be substituted for the blue with delicious results.

Serves 4

COST: Moderate

PREP TIME: 5 minutes

START-TO-FINISH TIME:
15 minutes

3 tbsp olive oil

18 oz/495 g pre-washed fresh baby spinach

3 oz/90 g blue cheese, crumbled,
  or creamy goat cheese (see market note)

Kosher salt (optional)

4 tsp coarsely chopped hazelnuts

1. Heat the olive oil in a large, heavy frying pan set over medium-high heat. When the oil is hot, add one-third of the spinach and stir constantly until the spinach begins to wilt. Add another third and stir again until it wilts, then repeat with the remaining spinach. This whole process should take about 4 minutes. (The spinach can be sautéed 30 minutes ahead; leave uncovered at room temperature. Reheat over medium heat until hot.)

2. Remove from the heat, and if any liquid has accumulated in the pan, carefully pour it off and discard. Add half of the cheese to the spinach, and stir a few seconds just until the cheese begins to melt. Taste and season with salt. Divide the spinach into 4 servings and garnish each with a sprinkle of the remaining blue cheese and the chopped hazelnuts.

MARKET NOTE: If using blue cheese, Bleu d'Auvergne works particularly well. If using goat cheese, a creamy variety is the best choice.

SERVE WITH: Try this spinach with Roast Veal with Tarragon-Mustard Butter (page 81), or use goat cheese in place of the blue cheese and serve it with Boneless Leg of Lamb with Tomato-Olive Relish (page 71).

5-Minute Roasted Sugar Snap Peas

For a recipe that calls for only four ingredients, including oil and sea salt, this dish delivers great flavor and requires just a small investment of your time. Because of their simplicity, the peas are also incredibly versatile. Talented young cook Kirsten Wilson shared this inventive recipe with me.

Serves 6

COST: Inexpensive

PREP TIME: 10 minutes

START-TO-FINISH TIME: 15 minutes

1 lb/455 g sugar snap peas, trimmed

1 tbsp olive oil

Fleur de sel

1 to 2 tbsp minced chives (optional)

1. Arrange a rack 4 to 5 in/10 to 12 cm from the broiler/grill and preheat the oven to broil/grill. Line a large, heavy baking sheet/tray with foil.

2. Place the peas on the baking sheet/tray and toss with the oil, and then spread them in a single layer.

3. Place the peas under the broiler/grill and broil/grill for 2 minutes. Remove the pan from the oven and turn the peas over with a metal spatula. Return the pan to the oven and broil/grill for about 2 minutes longer, until the peas are just lightly charred. Transfer the peas to a serving bowl and sprinkle them with fleur de sel (about ½ tsp or less). Garnish the sugar snaps with minced chives, if desired.

SERVE WITH: These peas can be served with all manner of roasts. Try them with Cumin-Rubbed Pork Tenderloins with Fresh Peach Salsa (page 46); with Ham Roasted with White Wine, Shallots, and Carrots (page 64); or with Sesame-Coated Tuna Steaks with Orange-Sherry Mayo (page 123).

Spring Vegetables Tossed in Spring-Herbs Butter

A colorful quartet of spring vegetables–turnips, carrots, peas, and sugar snaps—are quickly blanched, then tossed in a flavorful butter scented with tarragon and mint. The butter can be prepared a day ahead, and the vegetables blanched an hour in advance so that all that is necessary at serving time is a quick assembly and reheating.

Serves 8

COST: Inexpensive

PREP TIME: 25 minutes, including making the butter

START-TO-FINISH TIME: 35 minutes

Kosher salt

2 cups/340 g sliced carrots, peeled and cut on the diagonal into slices ⅛ in/3 mm thick

2 cups/340 g diced white turnips, peeled and cut into ½-in/12-mm cubes

2 cups/225 g sugar snap peas, ends trimmed

2 cups/305 g shelled fresh peas or frozen peas, defrosted

½ recipe Spring-Herbs Butter (page 172)

2 tsp minced fresh tarragon

2 tsp minced fresh mint

Fleur de sel

1. Bring a large pot of salted water to a boil and add the carrots and turnips; cook for 2 minutes. Add the sugar snaps and if you are using them, the fresh peas; cook until all the vegetables are tender, for about 2 minutes or more.

2. Drain the vegetables and return them to the same pot. If you are using defrosted frozen peas, stir them in. (The vegetables can be prepared 1 hour ahead; let rest at room temperature.)

3. Stir the Spring-Herbs Butter, tarragon, and mint into the vegetables and place the pot over low heat. Heat, stirring, until the butter has melted and the vegetables are heated through, for about 2 minutes. Season the vegetables with fleur de sel and mound in a serving bowl.

SERVE WITH: This dish makes an outstanding garnish to Orange-Studded Leg of Lamb (page 68), especially since both are prepared with the same herbed butter. These vegetables would also make a tempting side to Ham with an Orange Marmalade Glaze and Rhubarb Chutney (page 63).

Green Beans with Caramelized Shallots

When I was growing up, my mother prepared green beans only one way. She simmered them slowly in a big pot of water with onions and a hint of bacon drippings. Imbued with the flavor of onions and pork, these beans tasted great, but their army-fatigue green hue as well as the grayish tint of the onions left something to be desired. In the following recipe, the same flavoring principles apply—tender green beans are paired with shallots, another member of the onion family. However, these beans, blanched for only a few minutes until tender, retain their deep, verdant color. The shallots, sautéed in butter until they are a rich caramel brown, make a lovely visual contrast.

Serves 8

COST: Inexpensive to Moderate

PREP TIME: 15 minutes

START-TO-FINISH TIME: 45 minutes

1 lb/455 g shallots

2 tbsp unsalted butter

2 tbsp olive oil

¼ tsp dried thyme leaves

Kosher salt

Freshly ground black pepper

2 lb/910 g tender green beans, preferably haricots verts, trimmed (see market note)

Fleur de sel (optional)

MARKET NOTE: Haricots verts, the slim tender little green beans with the French name, are available in some supermarkets. If you can't find them, tender young green beans are fine. Haricots verts need to be cooked only about 5 minutes, while tender young green beans will need a couple of minutes more.

SERVE WITH: Try these with Standing Rib Roast with Porcini Mushroom Sauce (page 23), Golden Cider-Roasted Turkey (page 99), "Never Fail" Roast Turkey with Shallot Pan Gravy (page 102), or Crown Roast of Pork with Tarragon-Mustard Butter (page 52).

1. Cut off and discard the ends of each shallot. Halve lengthwise and, using a sharp paring knife, peel the skins from the shallots. If the shallots are large, quarter them lengthwise.

2. In a large, heavy frying pan, heat the butter and oil over medium-high heat until the butter is melted. When hot, add the shallots and stir a few seconds to coat well. Reduce the heat to medium-low. Cook the shallots, stirring frequently, until they are nicely browned, translucent, and tender, for 20 to 25 minutes; watch carefully so they do not burn. Season the shallots with thyme, ¼ tsp kosher salt, and several grinds of pepper. (The shallots can be prepared 4 hours ahead. Leave at cool room temperature and cover loosely with foil. Reheat over low heat, stirring.)

3. Cook the green beans in a large pot of boiling salted water until tender, for 4 to 6 minutes, depending on size. Drain them in a colander and then season with salt and pepper. Mound the beans in a shallow serving bowl and spoon the shallots over them. If desired, sprinkle both with a little fleur de sel.

Quick Skillet Corn Bread

This corn bread takes 20 minutes to assemble and bake, and will yield 4 cups/220 g of crumbs. You need 2 cups/110 g for the stuffing; freeze the extra for future use.

Serves 6 as a side

COST: Inexpensive

PREP TIME: 5 minutes

START-TO-FINISH TIME: 20 minutes

4 tsp vegetable oil

2 large eggs

¾ cup/180 ml buttermilk

¾ tsp baking powder

¾ tsp kosher salt

¼ tsp baking soda/bicarbonate of soda

1 cup/140 g yellow cornmeal

1. Arrange a rack at center position and preheat the oven to 450°F/230°C/gas 8.

2. Pour the oil into an 8- or 9-in/20- to 23-cm cast iron or heavy, ovenproof frying pan. Place the pan in the oven to heat for 3 to 4 minutes.

3. Whisk the eggs and buttermilk together in a large bowl. Whisk in the baking powder, salt, baking soda/bicarbonate of soda, and cornmeal. Remove the frying pan from the oven and carefully pour the hot oil into the batter. Whisk to combine. Pour the batter into the hot frying pan and bake until a tester comes out clean, for about 15 minutes.

4. Cool the corn bread and then break into chunks. Process into coarse crumbs in a food processor.

SERVE (AS A SIDE) WITH: This corn bread would be delicious with Racks of Pork with Apple Chutney (page 57) or Roasted Beef Short Ribs in Barbecue Sauce (page 40).

Skillet Summer Corn

In the summer when corn is so abundant that you see it piled high at roadside farm stands or tumbling out of bins at the supermarket, buy a few ears to make this vivid and easy side dish. Shaved kernels are sautéed with sweet onions until both are lightly caramelized, and then they are combined with bell peppers, chopped tomatoes, and fresh basil. Serve the corn straight from the frying pan or in a serving bowl.

Serves 4

COST: Inexpensive

PREP TIME: 25 minutes

START-TO-FINISH TIME:
40 minutes

3 tbsp unsalted butter

½ cup/65 g chopped sweet onion, such as
   Spanish or Vidalia

2 cups/290 g fresh corn kernels
   (cut from 3 to 4 ears)

Kosher salt

Freshly ground black pepper

½ cup/65 g chopped orange or
   red bell pepper/capsicum

½ cup/55 g sugar snap peas, ends trimmed
   and halved crosswise on the diagonal

¾ cup/150 g chopped tomatoes,
   seeded and stemmed

2 tsp balsamic vinegar (optional)

¼ cup/10 g julienned fresh basil

1. In a large, heavy frying pan (with a lid) set over medium heat, melt the butter until hot. Add the onion and sauté, stirring, until translucent, for 2 to 3 minutes. Add the corn and sauté, stirring often, until both the corn and onion start to caramelize, for 4 to 5 minutes. Season generously with salt and pepper.

2. Stir in the bell pepper/capsicum and sugar snap peas, then cover the frying pan and cook until the peppers and peas just start to soften, for about 3 minutes.

3. Remove the pan from the heat and stir in the tomatoes. Season with salt and pepper. Taste the mixture, and if you want to it to have a sharper flavor, stir in the balsamic vinegar. Serve the corn in the frying pan or mound it in a shallow serving bowl, and sprinkle with basil.

SERVE WITH: This corn would be delicious with Sesame-Coated Tuna Steaks with Orange-Sherry Mayo (page 123) or Skewered Shrimp with Warm Citrus Butter (page 133).

Wild Rice with Roasted Grapes and Walnuts

This dish is visually striking with its sleek dark grains of wild rice studded with bursts of color from red and green grapes. There's an interesting contrast of textures too—both wild and brown rice and some walnuts provide crunch, while the roasted grapes are juicy and soft. This recipe serves twelve, so it is a perfect accompaniment to a big roasted bird.

Serves 12

COST: Moderate

PREP TIME: 25 minutes, including toasting the walnuts

START-TO-FINISH TIME: about 2 hours

6 tbsp/85 g unsalted butter

1 cup/100 g chopped shallots

1 cup/115 g chopped celery

2 cups/430 g wild rice

5 cups/1.2 L chicken broth, plus more if needed

1 tbsp dried thyme

Kosher salt

1 cup/215 g brown rice

1½ cups/225 g red seedless grapes

1½ cups/225 g green seedless grapes

2 tbsp olive oil

1½ tsp balsamic vinegar

1 cup/115 g walnuts, toasted and chopped

1 tbsp grated orange zest

SERVE WITH: This beautiful rice would make a glorious side dish to Golden Cider-Roasted Turkey (page 99); "Never Fail" Roast Turkey with Shallot Pan Gravy (page 102); Turkey Breast with Cremini, Porcini, and Pancetta Stuffing (page 106); or as a filling for Crown Roast of Pork with Tarragon-Mustard Butter (page 52).

1. In a large, heavy pot (with a lid) melt the butter over medium heat until hot. Add the shallots and celery. Stir and cook until softened, for about 8 minutes. Add the wild rice and stir to coat with the butter. Add 5 cups/1.2 L of the broth, the thyme, and 1½ tsp salt and bring the mixture to a simmer. Cover and cook for 30 minutes. Add the brown rice and cover and cook for 40 to 50 minutes more, or until all liquid has been absorbed and the rice is tender but still has a little bit of crunch. If necessary, you can add ¼ cup/ 120 ml or slightly more broth to finish cooking the rice. (The rice can be prepared 1 day ahead. Cool, cover, and refrigerate. Reheat, stirring, over medium-low heat.)

2. While the rice is cooking, prepare the grapes. Arrange a rack at center position and preheat the oven to 350°F/180°C/gas 4.

3. Place the grapes on a large, rimmed baking sheet/tray and drizzle them with the oil; using a wooden spoon, stir to coat well. Roast, stirring once, until the grapes begin to wrinkle and some have collapsed, for about 15 minutes. Remove them to a bowl and toss with the balsamic vinegar. (The grapes can be prepared 4 hours ahead; leave at room temperature.)

4. Stir the walnuts, orange zest, and the grapes and their juices into the rice. Season with salt. Serve the rice mounded in a large shallow bowl.

Yorkshire Pudding with Bacon and Sage

A classic British side dish to roast beef, Yorkshire pudding is prepared with a simple popover-type batter of eggs, flour, milk, and butter, to which pan drippings are added. In this version, the usual beef drippings are replaced with smoky bacon, while another boost of flavor comes from minced fresh sage. The pudding, baked in a shallow pan, puffs up dramatically around the sides while it is in the oven and takes on a rich golden color. The Yorkshire in the name is for one of England's northern counties where this pudding originated.

Serves 8

COST: Inexpensive

PREP TIME: 10 minutes

START-TO-FINISH TIME:
1 hour

7 or 8 bacon slices (about 6 oz/170 g),
    cut into 1-in/2.5-cm pieces

2 tbsp unsalted butter, melted (if needed)

1½ cups/175 g flour

3 tbsp minced fresh sage

1 tsp kosher salt

1½ cups/360 ml whole milk

3 large eggs

1. Arrange a rack at center position and preheat the oven to 450°F/230°C/gas 8.

2. In a large, heavy frying pan set over medium heat, fry the bacon until crisp. Remove with a slotted spoon to drain on paper towels/absorbent paper. Transfer the bacon drippings to a heat-proof measuring cup to yield ¼ cup/60 ml. (If necessary, add enough melted butter to make this amount.) Pour the drippings into a 9-by-13-in/23-cm-by-33-cm baking dish and place it in the oven to heat the drippings for 10 minutes.

3. In a medium bowl, mix together the flour, half of the sage, and salt. In a large bowl, whisk together the milk and eggs. Whisk the flour mixture into the egg mixture until no lumps remain and the mixture is smooth. Stir in two-thirds of the bacon pieces.

4. Remove the hot baking pan from the oven and, using mitts or potholders (so that you do not burn yourself), tilt the pan several times to spread the drippings evenly over the bottom. Pour the batter into the pan.

5. Bake for 15 minutes, and then reduce the heat to 350°F/180°C/gas 4. Continue to bake until the pudding is golden brown and puffed, for 12 to 15 minutes more. When done, the sides will have puffed way above the edges of the pan. Do not open the door while baking.

6. Remove the pudding from the oven. Sprinkle the remaining bacon and sage over the pudding.

COOKING TIP: If you plan to serve the Standing Rib Roast with Porcini Mushroom Sauce (page 23) with this Yorkshire pudding, you can easily coordinate the two dishes. During the last 30 minutes of roasting the beef, cook the bacon and prepare the batter for the pudding. Remove the cooked roast and tent it with foil. While the roast is resting, center the rack in the oven and raise the temperature to 450°F/230°C/gas 8. Place the dish with the drippings in the oven for 10 minutes. Add the batter and bake the pudding. Since the roast needs to rest for 35 to 40 minutes, it will be ready to carve when the pudding comes out of the oven.

SERVE WITH: The Standing Rib Roast with Porcini Mushroom Sauce (page 23) is the ideal roast to pair with this side. It would also be delicious with Pepper-Crusted Sirloin Roast with Horse-radish Crème Fraîche (page 26).

Sourdough Dressing with Roasted Root Vegetables

A glorious array of roasted root vegetables distinguishes this bread dressing from others. They add bursts of color and a slight caramelized sweetness to the dish. Don't let the long list of ingredients keep you from trying this delectable dressing. The vegetables can be roasted and the sourdough bread cubed and toasted a day ahead, so that at serving time a quick assembly and baking is all that is necessary.

Serves 10

COST: Inexpensive

PREP TIME: 30 minutes

START-TO-FINISH TIME:
2 hours, 30 minutes

6 cups/255 g ½-in/12-mm sourdough bread cubes (without crust)

10-oz/280-g bag frozen pearl onions (see market note)

¾ lb/340 g carrots, peeled and cut into slices ½ in/12 mm thick

¾ lb/340 g parsnips, peeled and cut into slices ½ in/12 mm thick

¾ lb/340 g rutabagas/swedes, peeled and cut into ½-in/12-mm cubes

⅔ cup/165 ml olive oil

Kosher salt

Freshly ground black pepper

1 lb/455 g cremini/brown mushrooms, cleaned and, if large, halved

6 large garlic cloves, peeled

2 tsp dried thyme

2 tsp dried crushed rosemary (see cooking tip, page 19)

1½ tsp dried sage leaves, crumbled

3 tbsp unsalted butter, melted, plus more for greasing the baking dish

1½ cups/360 ml reduced-sodium chicken broth, plus more as needed

3 large eggs

1. Arrange a rack at center position and preheat the oven to 325°F/165°C/gas 3. Spread the bread cubes on a rimmed baking sheet/tray, and bake until dry and lightly browned, tossing once or twice, for 20 to 25 minutes. (The bread can be toasted 1 day ahead; cool, cover, and keep at room temperature.)

2. Arrange one rack at top position and another at lower position and raise the oven temperature to 425°F/220°C/gas 7.

3. Place the onions, carrots, parsnips, and rutabagas/swedes on a large rimmed baking sheet/tray and toss with half of the oil. Spread them in a single layer and season generously with salt and pepper. Place the mushrooms and garlic on another rimmed baking sheet/tray and toss with the remaining oil. Spread them in a single layer and salt and pepper generously.

4. Roast the onions, carrots, parsnips, and rutabagas until tender and brown around the edges, stirring every 15 minutes, for about 50 minutes. Roast the mushrooms and garlic until tender, stirring once, for 20 to 30 minutes.

5. Combine the vegetables and the mushrooms in a large bowl. In a small bowl, smash the roasted garlic cloves with a fork until pureed. Add the mashed garlic, thyme, rosemary, and sage to the vegetables and toss to combine. Season with salt and pepper. (The vegetables can be prepared 1 day ahead; cool, cover, and refrigerate.)

6. Arrange a rack at center position and reduce the heat to 375°F/190°C/gas 5. Butter a 9-by-13-in/23-by-33-cm or similar-size baking dish.

7. Add the bread cubes to the vegetables. In a medium bowl, whisk together the broth, eggs, and 3 tbsp butter, and stir into the vegetables until all the liquids have been absorbed and the mixture is moist. If necessary, add extra broth. Spread the dressing in the prepared dish and bake until lightly browned and crisp on top, for about 35 minutes.

MARKET NOTE: Frozen pearl onions, which are peeled and ready to use, work fine in this recipe and are a big time-saver. Avoid frozen ones in a cream sauce. Defrost and pat them dry before using.

SERVE WITH: This is a perfect side to Golden Cider-Roasted Turkey (page 99); "Never Fail" Roast Turkey with Shallot Pan Gravy (page 102); or Turkey Breast with Cremini, Porcini, and Pancetta Stuffing (page 106).

EXTRAS

Chutneys, Relishes, Seasoned Butters—
Great Flavor Bonuses

It's the extras—the glistening chutneys, the bracing salsas, the tangy relishes, the aromatic butters—that make roasts complete. They play an essential role, contributing contrasting flavors and textures and bursts of color. If a roast could be compared to that classic wardrobe item, the little black dress, then these extras would be the must-have accessories—the perfect jewelry and whiff of perfume.

Fruit chutneys with their spicy, sweet, and tart flavorings are superb partnered with lamb, turkey, and pork. Both Golden Cider-Roasted Turkey and "Never Fail" Roast Turkey with Shallot Pan Gravy taste even more inviting when topped with spoonfuls of Cranberry and Dried Cherry Chutney. Roast racks of pork served with glorious Apple Chutney create a symphony of textures, flavors, and colors.

Salsas and relishes are beautiful accompaniments to many other roasted main dishes, such as Cumin-Rubbed Pork Tenderloins with Fresh Peach Salsa and Boneless Leg of Lamb with Tomato-Olive Relish. Homemade Barbecue Sauce and Provence's famous garlic mayo, Aioli, are other condiments that enhance roasted specialties.

Seasoned butters often play dual roles: They baste meat, fish, and poultry while roasting, and then are spooned atop the cooked slices as a garnish. Spring-Herbs Butter is employed both to baste and embellish a leg of lamb, and Tarragon-Mustard Butter plays the same roles for a top loin of veal and a crown roast of pork.

Accessorize, accessorize, the fashion world declares. The same mantra works in the kitchen. Don't forget those special extras that turn a basic roast into a dazzling ensemble.

Apple Chutney

My longtime assistant and friend, Emily Bell, is the queen of chutneys. I've never been to her house when she didn't pull a new creation from her pantry. This apple chutney, which she invented one fall, is one of my favorites. Diced Gala apples, with their bright red skins left on, are simmered with onions and spices in a mixture of sugar and vinegar. Sweet, tart, and peppery, this chutney never fails to delight.

Makes about 1½ cups/ 400 g

COST: Inexpensive

PREP TIME: 15 minutes

START-TO-FINISH TIME: 45 minutes, plus 15 minutes or more for the chutney to cool

2 large Gala apples, unpeeled

3 tbsp olive oil

1 cup/125 g chopped onion

1 tsp minced garlic

⅔ cup/130 g light brown sugar

2 tsp country-style Dijon mustard

2 tsp minced fresh ginger

¾ tsp ground coriander

¼ tsp ground cinnamon

Generous pinch of cayenne pepper

⅓ cup/165 ml cider vinegar

1. Halve and core the apples, then cut them into ½-in/12-mm dice.

2. In a medium, nonreactive saucepan, heat 2 tbsp of the oil over medium heat. Add the onions and garlic and sauté, stirring, until onions are softened, for about 3 to 4 minutes.

3. Add the remaining 1 tbsp oil to the saucepan and stir in the diced apples. Sauté, stirring frequently, until the apples are translucent and lightly browned, for 5 to 6 minutes. Add the brown sugar, mustard, ginger, coriander, cinnamon, and cayenne and stir until the sugar starts to melt. Add the vinegar and bring the mixture to a simmer. Cook, stirring frequently, until the mixture thickens and the liquids are syrupy, for 10 to 12 minutes. Remove the pan from the heat and let the chutney cool to room temperature. (The chutney can be prepared 3 days ahead; cool, cover, and refrigerate. Bring to room temperature for 30 minutes before using.)

SERVE WITH: This recipe is called for in Racks of Pork with Apple Chutney (page 57) and would also make a splendid counterpoint to roast poultry and lamb.

Rhubarb Chutney

There are more ways to use rhubarb than in a fruit pie. It's absolutely delicious prepared as a savory condiment. When spring rhubarb appears, I dice the deep-pink stalks and cook them in a mixture of sugar, vinegar, and aromatic spices until they turn into a thick, glistening chutney.

Makes about
4 cups/1.1 kg

COST: Inexpensive

PREP TIME: 20 minutes

START-TO-FINISH TIME:
30 minutes, plus
1 hour, 15 minutes for
the chutney to chill

1 cup/200 g plus 2 tbsp sugar

½ cup/120 ml red wine vinegar

2 cinnamon sticks, broken in half

1½ tbsp minced fresh ginger

1½ tsp grated orange zest

Scant ½ tsp ground cardamom

4½ cups (about 1¾ lb)/ 800 g rhubarb,
   trimmed and cut into ½-in/12-mm dice

¾ cup/120 g dried currants

4 green/spring onions including all but
   2 in/5 cm of green stems, chopped

1. In a large, heavy saucepan, place the sugar, vinegar, cinnamon stick halves, ginger, orange zest, and cardamom and set over medium heat. Cook, stirring, until the sugar dissolves and the mixture comes to a boil.

2. Add the rhubarb, currants and green/spring onions; bring to a boil again. Reduce the heat and simmer until the rhubarb is tender but not falling apart, for about 4 minutes. Cool to room temperature and discard the cinnamon stick halves. Cover and refrigerate the chutney until it is cold and thickened, for at least 1 hour. (The chutney can be made up to 2 days ahead; keep refrigerated. Bring to room temperature before serving.)

SERVE WITH: This versatile chutney accompanies the Ham with an Orange Marmalade Glaze and Rhubarb Chutney (page 63) and also makes an ideal garnish to roasted lamb, pork, chicken, or turkey.

Cranberry and Dried Cherry Chutney

This deep crimson chutney is a favorite of my students. I've included it more than once in my Thanksgiving classes, and each time it turned out to be one of the most popular dishes on the menu. Everyone loves the balance of flavors–the sweetness of the cherries countered by the tartness of the cranberries.

Makes about 2 cups/ 585 g

COST: Inexpensive

PREP TIME: 10 minutes

START-TO-FINISH TIME: 25 minutes, plus 2 hours for the chutney to chill

1 cup/200 g granulated sugar

2 cups/225 g fresh cranberries

½ cup/80 g dried cherries

2 tbsp cider vinegar

1 tbsp light brown sugar

2½ tsp minced fresh ginger

1 cinnamon stick, broken in half

2 tsp grated orange zest

1. In a medium, heavy saucepan combine 1 cup/240 ml water and the granulated sugar and set over medium-high heat. Stir until the sugar has dissolved, and then bring the mixture to a boil without stirring.

2. Add the cranberries, cherries, vinegar, brown sugar, ginger, and cinnamon stick halves and stir to mix. Bring the mixture to a simmer, then lower the heat slightly and cook until the mixture just starts to thicken, for 6 to 7 minutes. Remove the pan from the heat and stir in the orange zest. Using tongs or a slotted spoon, carefully remove and discard the cinnamon stick halves. Cool the mixture to room temperature, then cover and refrigerate for 2 hours so that the chutney will thicken. (The chutney can be prepared 3 days ahead; serve chilled or bring to room temperature for 30 minutes before serving.)

SERVE WITH: This chutney is a fabulous garnish for Golden Cider-Roasted Turkey (page 99); "Never Fail" Roast Turkey with Shallot Pan Gravy (page 102); and Turkey Breast with Cremini, Porcini, and Pancetta Stuffing (page 106).

Orange-Ginger Relish

Fresh, juicy orange segments are accented with peppery bits of ginger in this cool, bracing relish. Julienned red bell peppers and sliced red onions add both color and crunch to the mix. The success of this dish depends on knowing how to cut attractive segments from the oranges, so be sure to follow the guidelines for best results.

Makes about 2 cups/400 g

COST: Inexpensive

PREP TIME: 20 minutes

START-TO-FINISH TIME: 40 minutes

3 large navel oranges

½ cup/65 g red bell pepper/capsicum cut into fine julienne 1 in/2.5 cm long

½ cup/65 g thinly sliced red onion cut into strips 1 to 2 in/2.5 to 5 cm long

2½ tbsp minced cilantro/fresh coriander

2 tsp minced fresh ginger

2 tsp toasted sesame oil

½ tsp kosher salt

¼ tsp red pepper flakes

1. Grate enough zest from the oranges to yield 2 tsp and set aside. Starting at the top and using a good sharp knife, slice off the skin and white pith from each orange in strips, moving around the orange in a circular fashion. The pith is bitter so you want to make certain that all traces are cut off. Working over a medium, nonreactive bowl, remove the orange segments by holding the knife perpendicular to the peeled orange and cutting from the top to the bottom along one side of the membranes that enclose each segment. Repeat cutting along the membrane on the other side of the segment. The segment will slip out easily at this point.

2. Add the orange zest, bell pepper/capsicum, onion, cilantro/fresh coriander, ginger, sesame oil, salt, and red pepper flakes and gently mix with the orange segments. (The relish can be prepared 1 hour ahead; keep at cool room temperature.)

SERVE WITH: This relish is called for in the Salmon Side with Fresh Orange-Ginger Relish (page 129), and would also be a fine partner to roasted pork or chicken.

Tomato-Olive Relish

The flavors of the Mediterranean shine through in this enticing condiment prepared with grape tomatoes, kalamata olives, and seasonings of fresh basil and rosemary. This relish packs a big punch of flavor, but is surprisingly and pleasingly low in calories.

*Makes about
1¾ cups/275 g*

COST: Moderate

PREP TIME: 20 minutes

START-TO-FINISH TIME:
25 minutes

1 cup grape tomatoes, quartered lengthwise into thin slivers, but not seeded (5 oz/180 g)

½ cup pitted kalamata olives, cut lengthwise into thin slivers (2½ oz/75 g)

3 tbsp minced fresh basil

2 tsp minced fresh rosemary

1½ tbsp drained capers

1½ tsp fennel seeds, crushed

Scant ¼ tsp red pepper flakes

Combine the tomatoes, olives, basil, rosemary, capers, fennel seeds, and red pepper flakes in a medium, nonreactive serving bowl and mix well. (The relish can be prepared 3 hours ahead; cover and leave at cool room temperature.)

SERVE WITH: This relish is good with roast lamb, veal, and chicken. Savor it with Boneless Leg of Lamb with Tomato-Olive Relish (page 71) and Summertime Olive-Studded Roast Veal (page 82).

Fresh Corn Salsa

My friend Matt Sunderland, a talented chef who often teaches cooking classes with me, created this delectable condiment. A sauté of fresh corn kernels, bell pepper, and onion is combined with tomatoes and a hint of lime. The salsa can be prepared several hours ahead and will actually improve in flavor as it rests.

Makes about 1½ cups/315 g

COST: Inexpensive

PREP TIME: 20 minutes

START-TO-FINISH TIME: 30 minutes

2 tbsp olive oil

1 cup/145 g fresh corn kernels (from 2 large ears)

¼ cup/40 g finely diced red bell pepper/ capsicum

¼ cup/40 g chopped red onion

½ cup/100 g finely diced tomatoes, unpeeled with seeds and pulp removed

1 tbsp fresh lime juice, plus more as needed

½ tsp ground cumin

Kosher salt

Freshly ground black pepper

⅛ to ¼ tsp red pepper flakes

2 tbsp minced cilantro/fresh coriander

1. Heat 1 tbsp of the oil in a medium frying pan over medium heat until hot. Add the corn and sauté, stirring often, until the kernels begin to brown, for about 4 minutes. Add the red bell pepper/capsicum and onion and sauté, stirring, for 2 minutes more. Remove to a nonreactive bowl.

2. Add the tomatoes, lime juice, cumin, ½ tsp salt, several grinds of black pepper, red pepper flakes, and the remaining oil. Mix well. (The salsa can be prepared 6 hours ahead. Cover and refrigerate. Bring to room temperature for 30 minutes before using.) At serving time, stir in the cilantro/fresh coriander and season the salsa with salt and an extra squeeze of lime juice if desired.

SERVE WITH: This salsa makes a great garnish for roasted poultry, pork, and fish. It's a great partner to Chipotle-Rubbed Turkey Breast with Fresh Corn Salsa (page 104) and Swordfish Steaks with Fresh Corn Salsa (page 122).

Fresh Peach Salsa

Fresh diced peaches and chopped red onion are the primary ingredients in this vibrant salsa. Lime juice and zest along with minced jalapeños provide tart and hot notes respectively. Make this salsa in the summer when peaches are sweet and in their prime.

Makes about 1¾ cups/280 g

COST: Inexpensive

Prep time: 20 minutes

START-TO-FINISH TIME: 50 minutes, including 30 minutes for the salsa to marinate

3 medium yellow peaches, ripe but not too soft

⅓ cup/60 g chopped red onion

3 tbsp minced cilantro/fresh coriander, plus sprigs for garnish

1½ tsp grated lime zest and 2 tsp fresh lime juice, plus more juice as needed

2 tsp minced garlic

1 to 2 tsp minced jalapeño pepper, seeds and membranes removed

Kosher salt

Freshly ground black pepper

Peel the peaches (see cooking tip), and cut into ½-in/ 12-mm or smaller dice. Put in a medium, nonreactive bowl with the onion, cilantro/fresh coriander, lime zest and juice, garlic, jalapeño pepper, and ¼ tsp each salt and black pepper. Taste and, if desired, add additional salt and black pepper and up to 1 tsp more lime juice for a sharper taste. Marinate the salsa for at least 30 minutes. (Salsa can be prepared 2 hours ahead; leave at cool room temperature.)

COOKING TIP: To peel the peaches, bring a medium saucepan of water to a boil. Add the peaches for 60 seconds, then remove them with a slotted spoon and drain. When cool enough to handle, cut an X on the bottom of each peach and peel the skins off with a sharp paring knife.

SERVE WITH: This salsa accompanies Cumin-Rubbed Pork Tenderloins with Fresh Peach Salsa (page 46) and would also taste delicious with roast chicken or lamb.

Chunky Guacamole Salsa

There's something about this particular guacamole that makes me return to it time and again. Simple and quick, its balance of flavors and contrast of textures result in a very tempting combo. The testers for this book repeatedly voiced their delight with this recipe, declaring it one of their all-time favorite guacamoles. The avocados are diced, not mashed as in classic versions, then combined with chopped tomatoes and tossed in a piquant lime dressing scented with cumin.

Makes about 2½ cups/ 590 g

COST: Inexpensive

PREP TIME: 10 minutes

START-TO-FINISH TIME: 25 minutes

2 ripe avocados, soft but not mushy, cut into ¼- to ½-in/6- to 12-mm dice

2 large ripe plum tomatoes (about 6 oz/ 170 g total)

One 3-in-/7.5-cm-long jalapeño pepper

2 tbsp fresh lime juice

2 tbsp chopped shallots

2 tbsp minced cilantro/fresh coriander

1½ tsp ground cumin

½ tsp kosher salt

2 tbsp olive or vegetable oil

1. Put the avocados in a nonreactive mixing bowl. Halve the tomatoes, seed and stem them, then cut into ½-in/12-mm dice. Add to the mixing bowl.

2. Wearing rubber gloves, halve the jalapeño lengthwise and scrape out the seeds and veins. Mince the jalapeño and add to the bowl.

3. In a separate small bowl, mix together the lime juice, shallots, cilantro/fresh coriander, cumin, and salt. Whisk in the oil. Pour over the avocados and tomatoes and mix gently so that the avocados do not get mashed. Taste and add more salt if needed.

4. If not using immediately, cover the surface with plastic wrap/ cling film and leave at room temperature for up to 1 hour. (The salsa can also be refrigerated for up to 4 hours. Bring to room temperature for 30 minutes before serving.)

SERVE WITH: This is used as a topping for Roasted Cod with Tomatoes and Chunky Guacamole Salsa (page 118) and it could be offered instead of the corn salsa as a garnish for Chipotle-Rubbed Turkey Breast with Fresh Corn Salsa (page 104).

Quick and Easy Béarnaise Butter

This butter is a riff on classic béarnaise sauce and takes far less time and expertise to execute. For the latter, a cooked reduction of white wine vinegar, minced shallots, and tarragon is combined with egg yolks, and then cooked gently while melted butter is slowly incorporated. In this much easier version, a seasoned vinegar reduction needs only to be stirred into some softened butter. Unlike the sauce, which is a last-minute operation, béarnaise butter can be conveniently prepared a day ahead.

Makes about 1 cup/ 225 g

COST: Moderate

PREP TIME: 20 minutes

START-TO-FINISH TIME: 30 minutes

½ cup/50 g chopped shallots

½ cup/120 ml white wine vinegar

3½ tbsp/6 g minced fresh tarragon

3½ tbsp/6 g minced flat-leaf parsley

¾ cup plus 2 tbsp/200 g unsalted butter, at room temperature

Kosher salt

Coarsely ground black pepper

½ tsp grated lemon zest

1. Place the shallots, vinegar, half of the tarragon, and half of the parsley in a small saucepan. Simmer over medium-high heat until the vinegar has reduced to about 2 tbsp, for 3 to 4 minutes. Strain the mixture into a small bowl, pressing down on the solids to release any liquid. Discard the solids and cool the tarragon vinegar to room temperature.

2. Using a table fork, mix the butter, remaining tarragon and parsley, ½ tsp salt, several grinds of pepper, and lemon zest in a medium, nonreactive bowl. A little at a time, mix in the cooled tarragon vinegar. Continue to mix until the vinegar has been almost completely absorbed into the butter. Season with additional salt and pepper if desired. (The butter can be prepared 1 day ahead. Cover and refrigerate. Bring to room temperature before using.)

SERVE WITH: This butter accompanies the New York Strip Loin with Béarnaise Butter and Smashed Fingerlings (page 28) and would be delicious served mounded atop slices of roast lamb or chicken as well.

Spring-Herbs Butter

Fragrant fresh tarragon and mint are the key players in this simple composed butter. They lend color as well as bright, refreshing flavors to the melange. A hint of tarragon vinegar counters the butter's sweetness.

Makes about ½ cup/ 140 g

COST: Inexpensive

PREP TIME: 10 minutes

START-TO-FINISH TIME: 15 minutes

½ cup/115 g unsalted butter, at room temperature

2 tbsp minced fresh tarragon

2 tbsp minced fresh mint

1 tbsp tarragon vinegar

1 tsp kosher salt

In a medium bowl, use a fork to stir together the butter, tarragon, mint, vinegar, and salt until well blended. (The butter can be prepared 1 day ahead. Cover and refrigerate. Bring to room temperature before using.)

SERVE WITH: This butter is used to baste the Orange-Studded Leg of Lamb with Spring-Herbs Butter (page 68) and to flavor the Spring Vegetables Tossed in Spring-Herbs Butter (page 150). Also try it on roasted salmon fillets, roast chicken, and asparagus.

Tarragon-Mustard Butter

Although only a handful of ingredients is needed for this seasoned butter, they all work together to produce a rich, complex taste. Fresh tarragon and crushed fennel seeds offer a hint of anise flavor, while the heat of the mustard and the sharp accent of vinegar balance the sweetness of the butter.

Makes about ¾ cup/ 170 g

COST: Inexpensive

PREP TIME: 10 minutes

START-TO-FINISH TIME: 15 minutes

½ cup/115 g unsalted butter, at room temperature

4 tbsp/7 g minced fresh tarragon

1½ tbsp Dijon mustard

1 tbsp tarragon vinegar

1½ tsp fennel seeds, crushed

½ tsp kosher salt

In a medium nonreactive bowl, mix together the butter, tarragon, mustard, vinegar, fennel seeds, and salt until well blended. (The butter can be prepared 1 day ahead; cover and refrigerate. Bring to room temperature before using.)

SERVE WITH: This butter is a key flavoring for the Roast Veal with Tarragon-Mustard Butter (page 81) and the Crown Roast of Pork with Tarragon-Mustard Butter (page 52). It would also be delicious brushed on roasted salmon or chicken or as a seasoning for asparagus or fresh peas.

Aioli

Creamy, smooth, and ivory-hued, this garlic-scented mayonnaise is a specialty of Provence. It's a snap to make when you prepare it with a food processor; count on just 10 minutes to whip it up. If you don't have a food processor, follow the directions for the hand method in the cooking tip at the end of the recipe.

Makes about 2 cups/ 480 ml

COST: Inexpensive

PREP TIME: 10 minutes

START-TO-FINISH TIME: 15 minutes when using a food processor and slightly longer for the hand method

3 medium garlic cloves, peeled and minced

½ tsp kosher salt

2 large egg yolks plus 1 large egg, at room temperature (see note)

2 tbsp plus 1 tsp fresh lemon juice

Generous pinch cayenne pepper

¾ cup/180 ml olive oil

¾ cup/180 ml canola or vegetable oil

NOTE: There are uncooked eggs in this recipe. Food safety experts caution that consuming raw eggs can expose you to salmonella contamination. Immune-compromised patients, the very young, and the elderly should not eat raw eggs.

1. Use a fork to mash the garlic and salt together in a small bowl until the mixture resembles a coarse paste.

2. Place the egg yolks, egg, lemon juice, and cayenne pepper in the bowl of a food processor fitted with the metal blade. Process for several seconds until all ingredients are well blended. Combine the oils in a measuring cup with a spout. With the processor running, slowly add the oils in a thin stream through the feed tube until all the oil has been added and the mixture is thick and smooth. (Most processors have a small hole in the bottom of the feed tube that will dispense the oil automatically in a thin stream.) Add the garlic mixture and process for several seconds more.

3. Place the mayonnaise in a nonreactive serving bowl, cover, and refrigerate. (Mayonnaise can be prepared 2 days ahead; keep covered and refrigerated.)

COOKING TIP: For handmade mayonnaise, rinse a mixing bowl with hot water and dry it well. Add 3 yolks (instead of 2 yolks and 1 whole egg), the lemon juice, and cayenne. Very slowly, whisk in the oil a drop or two at a time. After ½ cup/120 ml has been added, start to add the oil in a very thin stream. Whisk in the garlic mixture.

SERVE WITH: This mayo is especially good with roasted fish and is called for in the Blue Heron's Striped Bass with Summer Herbs, Tomatoes, and Aioli (page 130). Use it for sandwiches made with leftover roast beef, lamb, chicken, or veal.

Homemade Barbecue Sauce

All the classic flavor notes—sweet, tart, hot, and spicy—can be found in this sauce. Although the ingredients are typical of those used in commercial barbecue sauces, this one is so much more complex and delicious. It can be prepared several days ahead and also freezes well.

Makes about 3 cups/ 810 g

COST: Inexpensive

PREP TIME: 20 minutes

START-TO-FINISH TIME: 1 hour

4 tsp canola oil

1 cup/125 g chopped onion

1 cup/280 g ketchup/tomato sauce

²/₃ cup/130 g packed light brown sugar

²/₃ cup/165 ml cider vinegar

¼ cup/60 ml unsulphured molasses/treacle

2 tbsp Worcestershire sauce

2 tbsp instant coffee powder

2 tsp yellow mustard

2 tsp chili powder

1 tsp ground cumin

¼ tsp ground cinnamon

¼ tsp cayenne pepper

In a large, heavy saucepan, heat the oil over medium heat. When hot, add the onion and sauté until translucent, for 4 to 5 minutes. Whisk in 1½ cups/360 ml water, the ketchup/tomato sauce, brown sugar, vinegar, molasses/treacle, Worcestershire sauce, coffee powder, mustard, chili powder, cumin, cinnamon, and cayenne pepper. Bring the mixture to a boil, stirring continuously. Lower the heat and simmer until the mixture has reduced to about 3 cups/810 g, for about 30 minutes. (The sauce can be prepared 5 days ahead; cool, cover, and refrigerate. It can also be frozen for up to 2 months. Defrost and reheat when needed.)

SERVE WITH: This sauce is called for in Four-Hour Roasted Pork Shoulder for Pulled Pork Sandwiches (page 55) and in Chili-Roasted Baby Backs with Homemade Barbecue Sauce (page 60). It's also delicious brushed on roast chicken.

THE ROAST DIRECTORY

MEAT CUT EQUIVALENTS

U.S.	U.K.
Bottom Sirloin	—
Brisket	Brisket
Chuck Steak Roast	Chuck/Braising Steak
Flank	Flank
Plate	—
Rib Roast	—
Round	Topside and Silverside
Shank	Leg
Short Loin, Sirloin, and Top Sirloin	Sirloin
Short Ribs	Thin Rib
Tenderloin	Fillet Steaks
—	Thick Rib

NOTE FOR UK READERS: If the cut a recipe calls for does not have an equivalent on the above chart, talk with your butcher about getting the best approximation of the meat cut.

ROASTS THAT NEED LESS THAN 30 MINUTES IN THE OVEN

Mini Wellingtons
37

Cumin-Rubbed Pork Tenderloins
with Fresh Peach Salsa
46

Pork Tenderloins with Cranberry–Port Wine Sauce
44

Veal Chops with a New Orleans Stuffing
84

Chicken Breasts Stuffed with Figs,
Prosciutto, and Gorgonzola
94

Roasted Cod with Tomatoes and
Chunky Guacamole Salsa
118

Halibut Steaks with Spinach, Chickpeas, and Bacon
120

Swordfish Steaks with Fresh Corn Salsa
122

Sesame-Coated Tuna Steaks
with Orange-Sherry Mayo
123

Skewers of Peppered Tuna with Wasabi Mayo
124

Salmon Fillets on a Bed of Peas
127

Salmon Side with Fresh Orange-Ginger Relish
129

The Blue Heron's Striped Bass
with Summer Herbs, Tomatoes, and Aioli
130

Skewered Shrimp with Warm Citrus Butter
133

Scallop Gratins with
Lemon-Garlic Bread Crumbs
135

ROASTS THAT NEED A LONG TIME IN THE OVEN (1½ HOURS OR MORE)

Old-Fashioned Pot Roast and Vegetables
with Extra-Rich Pan Gravy
18

Standing Rib Roast with Porcini Mushroom Sauce
23

Roasted Beef Short Ribs in Barbecue Sauce
40

Crown Roast of Pork with
Tarragon-Mustard Butter
52

Four-Hour Roasted Pork Shoulder
for Pulled Pork Sandwiches
55

Chili-Roasted Baby Backs with
Homemade Barbecue Sauce
60

Ham with an Orange Marmalade
Glaze and Rhubarb Chutney
63

Ham Roasted with White Wine,
Shallots, and Carrots
64

Corfu Lamb and Vegetables
Roasted in Parchment
72

Lamb Shanks with Dates and Olives
74

Veal Shanks Roasted in Red Wine
with Tomatoes and Sage
87

Bistro Roast Chicken with Garlic,
Onions, and Herbs
92

Golden Cider-Roasted Turkey
99

"Never Fail" Roast Turkey with
Shallot Pan Gravy
102

SHOWSTOPPER ROASTS FOR SPECIAL OCCASIONS

Standing Rib Roast with
Porcini Mushroom Sauce
23

New York Strip Loin with Béarnaise
Butter and Smashed Fingerlings
28

Beef Tenderloin with
Roasted Shallots, Bacon, and Port
32

Beef Tenderloin Stuffed with Spinach,
Mascarpone, and Sun-Dried Tomatoes
35

Crown Roast of Pork with
Tarragon-Mustard Butter
52

ROASTS THAT CAN BE SERVED AT ROOM TEMPERATURE

Rolled Flank Steak with a Corn Bread
and Chorizo Stuffing
30

Cumin-Rubbed Pork Tenderloins
with Fresh Peach Salsa
46

Ham with an Orange Marmalade Glaze
and Rhubarb Chutney
63

Summertime Olive-Studded Roast Veal
82

The Blue Heron's Striped Bass with
Summer Herbs, Tomatoes, and Aioli
130

ROASTS FOR HOLIDAYS

CHRISTMAS

Standing Rib Roast with Porcini Mushroom Sauce
23

Pork Tenderloins with
Cranberry–Port Wine Sauce
44

Crown Roast of Pork with
Tarragon-Mustard Butter
52

EASTER OR CHRISTMAS

Ham Roasted with White Wine,
Shallots, and Carrots
64

EASTER

Ham with an Orange Marmalade
Glaze and Rhubarb Chutney
63

Orange-Studded Leg of Lamb with
Spring-Herbs Butter
70

Racks of Lamb with New Potatoes
and Mint Pesto
76

Salmon Fillets on a Bed of Peas
127

THANKSGIVING

Golden Cider-Roasted Turkey
99

"Never Fail" Roast Turkey
with Shallot Pan Gravy
102

Turkey Breast with Cremini,
Porcini, and Pancetta Stuffing
106

ROASTS THAT WON'T BREAK THE BANK

Old-Fashioned Pot Roast and
Vegetables with Extra-Rich Pan Gravy
18

Roasted Beef Short Ribs in Barbecue Sauce
40

Four-Hour Roasted Pork Shoulder
for Pulled Pork Sandwiches
55

Chili-Roasted Baby Backs
with Homemade Barbecue Sauce
60

Bistro Roast Chicken with Garlic, Onions, and Herbs
92

Chicken Quarters Roasted with
Lemons and Green Olives
97

ROASTS FOR CALORIE COUNTERS

Summertime Olive-Studded Roast Veal
32

Cumin-Rubbed Pork Tenderloins
with Fresh Peach Salsa
46

Corfu Lamb and Vegetables Roasted in Parchment
72

Chicken Quarters Roasted
with Lemons and Green Olives
97

Chipotle-Rubbed Turkey Breast with Fresh Corn Salsa
104

Swordfish Steaks with Fresh Corn Salsa
122

Salmon Side with Fresh Orange-Ginger Relish
129

INDEX